Published by Bookman Projects Limited, 1 Canada Square,
Canary Wharf, London E14 5AP
First published 1995

ISBN 1-898718-60-1

Printed and bound in Great Britain by
BPC Hazell Books Ltd
A member of
The British Printing Company Ltd

CONTENTS

ACKNOWLEDGEMENTS

The authors would like to thank the following people
for their assistance and support in the
creation of this book:
James and Mary Doyle, Elizabeth and all the family,
Clive and Margaret Mowbray, Tommy Burns,
Davie Hay, Lou Macari, Jim Cassidy,
Peter Samson, Gerry Gallagher,
the library staff of the Daily Record and Sunday Mail,
the Middlesbrough Evening Gazette, Harry Glasper,
and for their unbelievable patience,
Pauline, Martin and Megan.

FOREWORD
by Jimmy Doyle,
Tony's father-in-law

I COULD tell Bernadette was up to something. My daughter had suddenly started showing an interest in Celtic Football Club and one day casually dropped into the conversation the question: 'Do you happen to know anything about Tony Mowbray?'

For years, I had been going to the occasional Celtic match with John McStay, the father of my son-in-law Willie and club captain Paul McStay. It was not as if I was a die-hard supporter or anything but perhaps because of my Irish upbringing, there was only ever one football team in Glasgow I would go and see.

Bernadette happened to mention that Tony Mowbray, a new signing at the club, had been coming to visit her quite a lot at work. It turned out that they had met one night in Glasgow and this was the player developing the early stages of courtship. I think Bernadette was asking me to find out about him. So, like any father concerned for the welfare of his daughter, I did.

I went to John McStay and he asked Paul what he knew about the big lad from the north east of England who had joined Celtic for £1million. Paul reported he was 'a proper gentleman, a really nice guy' and that was good enough for me. I know only too well that in these modern times, Mary and I had brought up our nine children in a very traditional manner, some would say strict.

For example, the girls were never allowed to be seen by their brothers in a state of undress, so that meant my daughters would have to go to the bathroom in the morning fully-clothed.

Many people may think that a more liberal attitude would be

appropriate in the 1990s but that is the way we wanted to run our household and I think every parent should have the right to decide that at least.

Anyway, I told Bernadette what John had said and I believe she took that as the green light to begin their relationship. The next thing I knew, they were going out together.

It was months before we got to meet him. Bernadette was determined to keep him well out of the way, so it was Christmas 1992 before he eventually came over to our house in Barrhead.

Because Celtic had a game over the festive period, it meant he faced having his meal in a hotel somewhere because he would not be allowed by the club to go back to his folks in Middlesbrough. My wife, Mary, insisted he came to us for dinner.

I remember Mary was running late with the Christmas dinner, not helped by the fact that Bernadette's new boyfriend was coming for the first time. She got into a terrible flap.

With pots boiling over and Mary's face getting redder and redder, we thought it best for half-an-hour to send Tony off to the home of one of my sons, just to keep the pressure off my wife for a wee while.

Anyway, she needn't have worried. We liked Tony from the very beginning. He was completely at ease with us as we sat and chatted about football, politics and the like . . . the kind of topics people use to get to know someone better.

The fact that Bernadette liked him should have been enough for us, anyway. She was a remarkably reliable judge of character; with Bernadette, she either liked you or she didn't. There were no grey areas.

The third youngest of my nine children, she was a bubbly, happy girl in her early years. I can see her now, the day Mary and I went up to her infants school to see how she was getting on. No sooner had she spotted you, than she was wrapped around your legs, clinging on for dear life.

She became more earnest as she moved into her teens. I suppose all young people go through a stage of attempting to find themselves and Bernadette was no different. When she did find herself, she discovered a girl of independent spirit, determined to make her way in the world and to see as much of that world as she possibly could.

Maybe she took her wanderlust from me; my job in shipping navigation has taken me all over the world and perhaps unwittingly I had kindled a desire in Bernadette to see the grand sights I had witnessed.

When she was 17 years old, she took herself off to Newquay in Cornwall for work. We were not happy but we did not expressly forbid her from going. When she told us she was going to America, I was aghast.

I know how dangerous a country it can be and things were made worse by the fact that she was travelling without a work permit. Mexicans might think nothing of standing on a street corner, waiting for a bus to take them to work but I was horrified that my own daughter could end up in that pool of cheap labour.

Mary and I made it clear that we were strongly against her trip. But she went, nonetheless. I spoke to her a couple of times on the telephone and we exchanged letters while she was in America. I offered her money, if she needed it, but she always refused, saying things were fine.

I found out later, she could have used an extra few bob but she was too proud or stubborn to ask for it.

So when, at the age of just 21, she discovered that she was suffering from breast cancer, it was only natural that Bernadette should try to keep her feelings to herself.

After undergoing several operations in hospital to remove the tumour, she shunned our visits. Even members of her own family, her own brothers and sisters, were told that she would rather not see anyone.

So as she slowly began to rebuild her life after that, it was fantastic to see the transformation which meeting Tony had on her personality. She was much more relaxed and eventually, so much in love.

It is hard to adequately convey the admiration we have for Tony Mowbray. Footballers, in general, do not enjoy the best of reputations. All we hear about are soccer stars ending up in court for brawling or facing allegations that they have taken money to 'fix' games.

But then if Tony Mowbray had been a 'normal' footballer, he would not have attracted my daughter in the first place.

Just like Bernadette, he had very firm views on how people should conduct themselves. Just like Bernadette, he didn't drink and he didn't smoke, and unlike many soccer stars I could name, he didn't chase after women.

When news hit us that Bernadette had terminal cancer, we could not have had a more solid rock to lean on. He was with her always. He would go out to train with Celtic in the morning, give as much as all the other players had to give on the training ground, and then he would be dutifully back at my daughter's side.

When she was in hospital, he would insist on bedding down at night beside her, his big frame cramped into one of those fold-down chairs. And he would be there for weeks on end, giving her sips of water or merely stroking her hand to make her feel better.

He wasn't sleeping; he wasn't eating. At one stage, he had lost 17lbs and looked like a shadow of his former self.

Yet, at home, when Bernadette had to be carried downstairs for yet another hospital appointment, I saw that man pick her up and take her to the waiting car. He simply wasn't up to the job but he would never ask someone else to carry her. To him, it was a pleasure.

I feel so deeply for him because of what he did for my daughter and for us. He took so much of the burden off me and

Mary and never once complained about it.

A father has to recognise that, some day, his girl is going to want to be with some man more than him. And Bernadette wanted so much to be with Tony.

He is an incredible guy. Had I been in his shoes, I am sure I would have cracked under the pressure.

To me, he is a born leader. Leadership, whether it is in football management or whatever, is about having understanding for the feelings of people.

That's why, if ever I was in a crisis and there were 20 men around me, I would shout on Tony Mowbray.

I am still hurt and shocked that he and Bernadette did not have more time together.

Believe me, they would have made some team.

DEDICATION

To Bernadette: I feel lucky and honoured to know that what we had and shared together in such a short time, some people never have in a lifetime.

Chapter One
My Mam and JFK

I HAD signed for Celtic for £1million but I hardly knew the first thing about Scotland, never mind the city of Glasgow. I was living on my own in the Albany Hotel and was terrified of the type of woman who tends to hang around footballers . . . the sort who are only after you for the lifestyle you might be able to offer them.

Then I met Bernadette Doyle. Here was a young woman who didn't have dyed blonde hair and didn't wear a Barbie dress. And she listened. She listened to me pouring my heart out about the fiancee I had left behind . . . about how I was so lonely in a big hotel in a city I did not know.

And after she had listened, she went back to her sister, Elizabeth and told her: ' It's fantastic. I've met someone just like me.'

That was the turning point in my life, which had begun on an infamous day in the early Sixties. Most people over the age of 35 can remember where they were the day I was born. Neil Kinnock was in the upstairs bar of the Globe Inn in Cardiff, 'lubricating' for a debate at his Students Union. Jackie Stewart was an up-and-coming young racing driver, predictably behind the wheel of a car between North Wales and his home in Dumbarton. Cliff Richard? I can tell you with some assurance he was taking a bath.

The reason I can be so precise about the whereabouts of these celebrities is because I happen to share my birthday with one of the most infamous acts of the 20th Century...the assassination of President John Fitzgerald Kennedy in Dallas.

22 November 1963. It always hits me when I hear people say they can remember where they were that day. I know where I

was. .I was just coming into this world. I've never really spoken to my mam about it but I suppose she must just have been getting on with it at the Saltburn Maternity Hospital near Redcar.

Looking back, I imagine some people could become obsessed by something like that, being born on a day that has become notorious for an act of evil. For me, there simply wasn't time. Childhood, to Anthony Mark Mowbray, meant football, football, football. Morning, noon and night.

I find it funny now when I drive around Glasgow and see kids playing among the most horrendous social conditions. That's the way it was with us on the Lakes Estate in Redcar. You didn't see the posh house half-a-mile up the road. All you saw was the ball in front of you and you went after it. That's why I don't feel too sorry for the kids I see today. They don't know any different.

As a lanky, long-haired lad, I constantly had a ball under my arm. I went to school with a ball every day for five years. Some of my friends were bewitched by computers; others fell under the spell of girls. Me? I would have my ball as I walked down to the shops in Redcar High Street, waltzing in and out of people out doing their shopping. If the other boys weren't around, I'd kick it against a garage door, kick it off a sea wall down on the beach or dribble it through some of my neighbours' gardens.

Football was just natural to me. Whether it came naturally as a result of all those hours I put in as a kid on a council estate, I don't know.

But I didn't just *want* to be a professional footballer; I needed to be.

There comes a stage in your life when you just know you are better than all the other kids on the pitch...you know you can slot the ball into the top corner when you want.

You know you can get the ball, dribble around eight or nine other kids and score a goal.

You have to worry when you see all these dads at matches, screaming at their sons, aching for their boy to be a professional footballer. But it's the kid himself who will know if he's good enough or not.

There's a definite rosy glow around those early days. I never came across anything nasty. It was pre-drugs and I was lucky never to see violence of any sort. If there was any badness around, it must have gone right over my head.

The most trouble I ever got into was the typical situation where the local bobby would take your name for being cheeky to an old woman, who refused to give you your ball back.

Yet for someone who has such warm memories of youth, it always seems to be winter whenever I look back. There's me standing in my mam's kitchen of our house at 48 Essex Close, big lumps of mud clinging to my trackie bottoms.

That's because I used to love throwing myself around in the mud, tackling and sliding into your opponent. I loved playing in goal . . . in fact that's how my nickname 'Mog' originated. Mog the cat.

At the Lakes Estate Junior School, I used to have a five-a-side team called 'Mogga's Marmalisers' and I was their energetic goalkeeper.

Football was really for the fourth year pupils but I managed to get some games in during first year and by the time I was in third year, I was captain of the school team.

We were winning cups and medals galore and it's around that time that one of my happiest memories occurred. We had just won the Redcar Cup and I, as captain, was presented to David Mills.

I just remember looking at him in his brown sheepskin coat and thinking 'this is David Mills of Middlesbrough F.C. and he's giving me the trophy.'

If football dominated my life outside school, maybe that's because it had intervened dramatically in the class as well. I was in the middle of studies at my infants school in 1972 and I remember all the kids turning to look at something unusual going on. It was my dad.

My mam was a dinner lady at the school and she has since told me she couldn't believe it as she saw her Clive walking right through the school with this purposeful look about him.He just came walking into the room, took me by the hand and we were off. I was totally bewildered as we walked out the school gates. We got into his red Corsair and he looked over to me, sat there, and said:'I'm going to take you to see Georgie Best, son.' I don't know if he even spoke to the teacher. Maybe he did.

It was Middlesbrough v. Manchester United in a replay of the fifth round of the F.A. Cup, the first 'proper' game I had ever been to. What still sticks in my mind is walking up the steps at Ayresome Park and, having got to a certain height, being astonished at the sight of the pitch. It was the greenest grass I had ever seen.

I know subsequently that Middlesbrough had a great reputation in those days for their playing surface. But this was a carpet, a stretch of ground too perfect for anything like football to be played on.

Manchester United won the game 3-0 but I always wondered why the game took place in the afternoon, during school hours. I know now that it was 29 February, slap-bang in the middle of the industrial war between the miners and Ted Heath's Tory Government. Power cuts, which had been going for nearly three weeks then, meant they couldn't use the floodlights at night.Little did I know then, but I would return to the Holgate End as a bigger boy to cheer on my Middlesbrough heroes, John Hickton and Alan Foggon. And then, years later, I would run out before that very crowd in the colours of the team I loved.

Strangely enough, while it was my dad who first took me to Ayresome Park, it may have been down to my mam that I ended up playing there as club captain.

I was in my last year at Lakes Junior School when a scout came to see me for the first time. I think the sports teacher had written to Middlesbrough to say there was someone worth having a look at.

The club sent along Ray Grant to watch me. He was a legend in those parts, a retired headmaster.....a lovely man who was really old even then.

It was a real event. The whole school was allowed out that afternoon to see the game... I remember we were playing a school called Newcombe in our new, blue jerseys with the old V-necks.

All the 10-year-olds were screaming their girlie screams and you were trying, through the crowds, to spot this mythical figure in a trench coat. You knew, too, that your parents were there – as if there wasn't enough pressure on you already!

Anyway, at half-time the score was nil-nil and I looked over to see my mam was crying. She knew Mr Grant was there and she was desperate for her son to do well.

I hadn't been doing too badly but I knew I had not been running the show the way I normally did. In any case, it was like a script from a Roy of the Rovers story in the second half. I scored all three goals and we ran out 3-0 winners.

After leaving the dressing room, I was told that Mr Grant had been very impressed by my performance and the club would be in touch. After all, this was Middlesbrough F.C. the only team that boys in that part of England dreamed of playing for.

Even up until the time I left for Celtic, I kept in touch with Mr Grant. He's in his 80s now but after all our games at Ayresome Park, he would come into the lounge afterwards and I'd make a point of going over to speak to him.

I would be out in my car after training and I'd always pull over whenever I'd see a football match. And Mr Grant would be stood there on the sidelines.

He always takes his wife to the match and she sits in the car and reads a book. Lovely, lovely people.

But back to my 'trial'. I couldn't get home quick enough to tell my mam that I had taken the first leap into my football career.

But it's funny that I can't remember her reaction when I told her.

All I remember are her tears at half-time.

Chapter Two
Graeme Souness and Born Again 'Boro

I STILL treasure a letter sent to my mam and dad by the headmaster of my comprehensive school, informing them of the dangers of aiming for a career in football.

My dad had been reading the riot act at Saltscar Comprehensive because while teachers wanted me to play rugby, he reckoned I might be good enough to become a professional footballer. The odd conflict of fixtures between my soccer sides and my school rugby was beginning to cause some friction.

After yet another visit to the school by my parents, headmaster Mr F.E.J. Corbett wrote to them on 27 September 1977:

'Dear Mr and Mrs Mowbray,

'With regard to the problem of Anthony's playing representative football, I have consulted with all the Games teachers together with the Head of Department for P.E. and Games.

'As I said yesterday, there is not a problem of affiliation. Also I do not object to boys of this Year Group playing representative Soccer UNLESS they are required for school (rugby) games. If there is a conflict of interests I consider that the school match should have priority, since we are not now playing Soccer as a recognised school game.

'Concerning your expressed conviction that this is a matter affecting Anthony's career prospects, I feel obliged to offer again my advice that there are many dangers involved in being sure, at this stage, that Anthony will make Football his career.

'He needs to direct his thoughts more to the academic and

general educational training which will offer him the chance of a secure future.

Yours sincerely

F.E.J. Corbett, Headmaster.

Later the same year, the school magazine carried a little story between 'Duke of Edinburgh Awards' and 'Chess Club News'. It read: 'SOCCER: A. Mowbray Y3 is to be congratulated on his selection for Cleveland County Schools U15 team.'

Thanks to the intense support of my mam and dad, I was beginning to make a name for myself in local, district and now county soccer teams.

They went to every match I played in, a habit they refused to shake off even when I turned pro.

In my early teenage years, I captained the Langbaurgh and Cleveland Under-15 sides. I also appeared for Grangetown Boys, Nunthorpe Athletic and Guisborough Town.

Although I was determined to play for 'Boro, my dad and I flirted with Aston Villa in 1977. I think my dad wanted me to see what another club looked like up close or maybe he didn't want Middlesbrough to think they were going to sign me as a matter of course, just because I was a 'Boro-mad local boy.

We went down to Birmingham at the invitation of Villa youth development officer, Dave Richardson. There, I met John Gidman and I was just one of several boys who insisted on having their photo taken with Villa's top man at the time, Andy Gray.

Fate intervened to prevent me facing Paul McStay as early as June 1980 when England welcomed Scotland's Schoolboys to Wembley for what turned out to be a classic match.

I had been selected for a trial for England Schoolboys, a practice match due to be held in Durham. It seemed a million miles away but it turns out it was only 40 minutes from my home in the car.

Anyway, I broke my leg within five minutes of the trial beginning and could only watch in agony. Many of the lads from that day went on to play in that classic 5-4 defeat by the Scots. Paul McStay, a Celtic S form signing at the time, scored with a ferocious shot from the edge of the box and then popped in another shortly after half-time. Whether he would have done that if I had been playing, I'll never know.

As a further coincidence, Graeme Souness was still at Middlesbrough when I signed associated schoolboy forms for the club on the day of my 14th birthday.

Never one to throw anything away, I've still got my original registration slip from the day I signed. It is numbered 12187.

And as a further coincidence, former Celtic legend Bobby Murdoch was the youth team coach then and he witnessed my signature.

But to simply say that Mowbray and Souness were now on the Middlesbrough playing staff is like saying the Pope and a small-town priest work for the Catholic Church.

And it is in such high regard that I held the man with the outrageous perm and bushy moustache . . . and in many ways still do.

He signed for 'Boro from Tottenham Hotspur in January 1973, captured for the princely sum of £30,000.

By the autumn of that year, the young Scot had made the Middlesbrough No.4 jersey his own. That top was special to the Ayresome Park faithful as it had been worn in the 1940s and 50s by Harry Bell and Bill Harris; it had been worn in the 1960s by Billy Horner, Stan Anderson and Don Masson and; it had been worn before Souness by one Nobby Stiles.

Souness was a god-like figure to us young ones, who would only report to Ayresome Park during the school holidays.

It was our chance to come within touching distance of the legends we saw on the park or read about in the local newspaper.

19

The apprentices would gossip about how Middlesbrough night clubs would pay Souness vast sums of money just to turn up on their premises a couple of nights a week.

We were so respectful that we addressed Souness and the rest of the first-team squad as 'Sir' and had to knock the door of their dressing room before we dared go in. Not like nowadays. The apprentices now are a cheeky lot of beggars.

I was such a small part in the grand scheme of things at Middlesbrough that I don't think I ever had a conversation with Graeme Souness.

But I do have a picture of him standing talking to boss Jack Charlton . . . and there's this youngster called Tony Mowbray, sitting in the background cleaning the boots.

Sure, he had an explosive start to his career with Rangers but you have to admit that Souness changed the Scottish game for good.

I know I missed his era but as far as I am concerned, he is still a figure to be respected.

I loved his style of play at Liverpool; to me he was everything a mid field player should be..committed and courageous. He was a born winner, ready to do anything to ensure his team won.

But a fellow professional can see a side to his game for which he's never really been given credit. He would protect other players in his team who were less dominant than he was.

Alright, he did some silly things at times. There were many tackles you could politely describe as 'rash' and he was known to lose the head on occasion.

But he was a protector . . . and that's what I admired most.

Kevin Keegan, his old mate from Liverpool, was my worthy opponent when I made my debut for the Middlesbrough first team. The date: 8 September 1982. The venue: that cauldron of north-east passion, St James's Park.

It was to be the first of over 400 appearances for the Ayresome

Park club. When I became club captain, I tried to emulate Graeme Souness both on and off the park. The quality of being willing to assume responsibility can act as a great encouragement to younger, more impressionable players. As the 'main man' if you like, I felt it my duty to guide and steer them through difficult patches, whether in a game or in their life.

I wanted Middlesbrough to come over in the right light so I would attend as many supporters' functions as I could.

And I would try to cushion less forceful members of the team from the worst excesses of 90-minute football.

Those players included names like Stuart Ripley, later to star in a £1.3 million signing to Blackburn Rovers, Colin Cooper, transferred to Nottingham Forest for £1.8 million and, of course, my mate Gary Pallister, who eventually moved to Manchester United in 1989 for a record defender's fee of £2.3 million.

I would like to think I helped in the development of all of those players, and maybe a few more.

When he first came to my attention, 'Pally' was the typical 'Bambi on Ice'. At six foot five inches tall, he looked so ungainly with those long pins we nicknamed him 'Inspector Gadget Legs'.

He could wrap those legs around anything that moved. I remember his head being turned when he discovered that Alex Ferguson might be interested in signing him for Manchester United.

He tried to push all thoughts of a transfer to the back of his mind and did very well on the park, considering. But eventually, after about a year of constant Press reports linking him to Fergie, he went in to chap the manager's door.

Middlesbrough were refusing to let him go. They wanted him to help maintain our battle for honours. I do remember the whole thing getting very messy, with Pally insisting he wanted to go and the club insisting that he was going nowhere.

But money talks and £2.3 million talks very loudly indeed. Fergie got his man, but as far as I am concerned, he also got a bargain. Moving to Manchester United has helped Pally progress from being a very good footballer to being a world-class footballer in a fairly short space of time. In my book, he's easily the best defender in Britain, if not Europe.

Apart from inspiring triumphs on the park with Liverpool, Bill Shankly is famous for the saying: 'Some people think football is a matter of life or death. I don't like that attitude. I can assure them that it is much more important than that.'

Well, if any of us actually believed that, then the tragic events of one fortnight in May 1985 forced us to put the game into true perspective.

It's hard to believe that in some sort of historical twist of fate, almost 100 lives were lost in football in just one two-week period 10 years ago. Liverpool supporters ran riot at the European Cup Final with Juventus, staged at the Heysel Stadium in Brussels.

Thirty-eight people died from their injuries as they tried to escape the charging masses.

And just a fortnight earlier, an unbelievable 56 people burned to death when fire raged through an old wooden stand at Valley Parade, the home of English Third Division side, Bradford City.

It turned out that the disaster had been caused by a dropped match or cigarette igniting a heap of paper which had been allowed to accumulate under the stand for over 20 years.

Like everyone else, I was stunned by the horrific TV pictures of people running for their lives, covered in flames.

But I felt really bad because I had played at Valley Parade many times in my career, right in front of the place where so many people perished.

On the day it happened, Saturday 11 May, Middlesbrough had travelled to Shrewsbury Town for the last game of the 1984/85 season. It was a match we had to win if we were to avoid relegation to the Third Division.

After the game, all the boys were in great spirits because we had beaten Shrewsbury 2-0 to stay up, but then someone listening to the radio on the bus home told us to be quiet.

Apparently, the spread of fire was so rapid, the entire stand was ablaze within four minutes of it starting.

The boys of Middlesbrough F.C. spent the rest of the journey home in stunned silence.

Very often, football people can get so caught up in their sport that they begin to believe Bill Shankly. But that just means that when terrible events like Heysel and Valley Parade and Hillsborough happen, the gut-wrenching feeling in the pit of the stomach is all the more acute.

But that is not to say that you cannot give the game your all; I built my reputation in England as a formidable defender who would stick his head where other players wouldn't put their boot!

Bruce Rioch, just one of the many managers I served in my years at Ayresome Park, paid me an astronomical compliment during our eventful season of 1988.

In a Press interview, Bruce happened to remark that I was such a good hand to have in a tight spot that if he ever travelled to the moon, he'd want Mogga with him!

He added: 'He takes genuine pride in what he does and is always prepared to lead by example. Apart from his physical attributes, he has tremendous inner strength.'

If I was pleased by his subsequent comments, it was his original remark about space flight that took off with the fans at Ayresome Park.

The club's first fanzine was launched on the back of that remark, appropriately-titled 'Fly Me to the Moon'. It's still going today.

But it's only fair that I return the compliment. Rioch, a former captain of Scotland's international side, did more than most to help restore respect both in and for Middlesbrough Football Club. Remember the dark days of 1986? The club went into liquidation and the gates of Ayresome Park were padlocked.

We were simply not a football club any more. All of the squad were given free transfers and we were all, effectively, left to fix up our own deals.

The players who still turned up had no training facilities to speak of; we were like little boys in the park, throwing track-suit tops and jumpers on to the ground to use as goal posts. We even brought along our own balls.

And with no-one else to cough up our cash, it was left to the borough council to pay our wages.

Here we were, professional footballers, in the habit of receiving our salary through the bank, and now turning up once a month at the town hall where a little old lady behind a desk would count out your money in front of you. And hand it over in £10 notes.

My best mate, Peter Beagrie, was one of the ones who moved on, managing to get a transfer to Sheffield United. But there was a small knot of players who were convinced that Middlesbrough Football Club could never go under.

Officially, they were already defunct. But somehow, in the back of your mind, you hope that a knight in shining armour is going to come charging into town at the eleventh hour and save the club you love. And that's exactly what happened.

Back in the Football League for the start of season 1986-87, we found ourselves in the Third Division, only the second time in Middlesbrough's history that we had been down there. Bruce Rioch had been appointed manager in February 1986, the run-in to our previous, cataclysmic season but had not quite managed to keep us up.

Now, we were playing in front of crowds of just 4,000. And because Ayresome Park was still padlocked, we had to play our first home game at The Victoria Ground, home of Hartlepool F.C.

As an even greater embarrassment, we had to wait until Hartlepool had played their home game before we could go out at 5.30 p.m. to face Port Vale in our first match as born-again

'Boro. Ironically, my mentor, Graeme Souness, was also making a fresh start on the first day of that season as manager of Glasgow Rangers.

The one thing that had not been lost in the near-evaporation of Middlesbrough's assets was Tony Mowbray's vast collection of superstitions...I had dozens of them and I made use of each and every one.

My main thing was insisting that I had to wear the No.4 jersey at Middlesbrough. This was regardless of whether I was on the bench, coming back from an injury or even out through suspension. No.4 was my jersey and no-one else was allowed to wear it. It was the jersey worn by Souness.

My pre-match meal had to consist of bacon toasties; then, getting changed, I would pull on my left boot before my right boot. My captain's armband stayed with me for years, just a simple sweat band someone had given me. And for the last six years I was at the club, I would insist on staying in the dressing room while the other players went through their warm-up on the pitch.

Then, just as we were taking the field, would come my piece de resistance. As we came out the tunnel, I would kick the ball 40 feet or 50 feet into the air and sprint on to the park, crucially before one foot had touched the grass. That became my hallmark at Middlesbrough and all the punters knew, when they saw that ball go skyward, that Tony Mowbray was on his way out.

Even after the game, I would go through a certain routine. The kit man, the late, great Ken, would always have two pints of chilled milk waiting for me coming off the park, just to settle my stomach.

The thinking behind these superstitions was simple; some sort of disaster would strike if they were not observed to the letter.

Anyway, I am sure they were all observed when we went out

for our first game at the Victoria Ground. And what should also be remembered was that we were all just kids. I think I was the oldest at 22 and five youngsters were given debuts that fateful day, August 23.

But we were being encouraged by Bruce's little sayings. He would quietly tell us in those dark days of the club's history: 'Out of adversity can come greatness.'

It seemed too good to be true when this motley collection of pro's and beginners were still 2-0 in the lead with 10 minutes to go.

Maybe my charms and amulets were working. Unfortunately, it *was* too good to be true. Port Vale scored a couple in the dying minutes to snatch a 2-2 draw.

But back in the dressing room, the new spirit of Middlesbrough F.C. was being born. Bruce Rioch came in and told us: 'That was their best shot. They've had a full pre-season programme to get ready for today.

'Port Vale have played in friendlies and they've enjoyed an organised training schedule. We've not been able to train because we've got no park and no balls. And still they couldn't beat you.'

Prophetically, he told us:'You can only get better. And better. And better.'

We soared on his words to an unbeaten run of 13 games at the start of the season, followed by an unbeaten run of 13 at the end.

Nine months after our re-birth at Hartlepool, in May 1987, we clinched promotion to the Second Division.

It may only have been a goal-less draw with Wigan but it signalled half-time in one of the greatest achievements ever by an English football club.

We were, by then, back at Ayresome Park and the sights that day will live with me for the rest of my life. I've still got the video, all those young lads standing on the ledge of the directors' box, waving to all our chanting fans on the park.

26

The next season, 1987-88, saw us go straight through the Second Division like a knife through butter.

It also saw Middlesbrough make impressive progress in the F.A. Cup, culminating in a series of dramatic Fourth Round encounters with Everton, the reigning First Division champions.

The first match had been drawn 1-1 at Goodison Park so the re-play switched to the Wednesday night at Ayresome Park, where we really fancied our chances. Everton were leading by one goal to nil and the clock was ticking away into injury time.

I remember the Middlesbrough fans were leaving the ground because they were convinced there was no way back for us.

Then we got a corner and in true Roy of the Rovers fashion (again!), I dashed to the near post to nod it in! In Middlesbrough, they still talk about the night when supporters half-way down Linthorpe Road heard the roar of the crowd acclaiming my equaliser. And how they came belting back up the road because they knew there was going to be another 30 minutes of extra-time.

The game finished 2-2, with Trevor Steven guaranteeing a third game, this time back on Merseyside, by equalising for Everton in the dying minutes.

The second re-play took place at Goodison Park on Tuesday, 9 February 1988. Stuart Ripley had kept our Cup dream alive by cancelling out Graeme Sharp's 19th goal of the season.

Conditions were absolutely horrendous as the wind and rain blew in remorselessly from the Irish Sea. Just six minutes were left when disaster struck. Gary Stevens (it had to be another Rangers player, didn't it?) whacked over a low cross which I dutifully converted into my own net by sticking out a despairing boot. The saint had become the sinner and after 300 minutes of competitive play against Everton, our dream of Wembley died in the mud of Goodison Park. It was Everton, and not us, who would go on to face the mighty Liverpool in the fifth round.

The following Sunday, battling 'Boro made their debut on live

TV as the first club outside of the recognised top-flight to be featured for a full 90 minutes on the box.

We were playing against Aston Villa, who were top of the Second Division at the time, on our home patch, Ayresome Park. It was a big game, which had received the usual build-up on telly during the week.

I remember I had a disastrous start, getting caught out on the touch line by Garry Thomson, one of their racier forwards. He cut inside me in the 36th minute and squared it for Tony Daley to slot it home.

But, perhaps making up for that mistake, I again chose the big occasion to score one of my 'specials'. Alan Kernaghan had pulled us equal within three minutes of coming on as a substitute when he struck home a shot Nigel Spinks had parried from Bernie Slaven.I don't know what I was doing up in the opposing penalty box four minutes later; maybe it was a free kick.

But whatever the reason for my presence there, I just remember Brian Laws whipping the ball in from the right and yours truly launching himself full-length from the penalty spot to head it low into the Villa net.

I hadn't given a thought to the stitches inserted at half-time after a clash of heads with Villa man, Martin Keown. Anyway, the scoreboard showed that there were just six minutes left when I struck...ironically exactly the same time that I scored my own-goal against Everton five days earlier!

The goal won me the Man of the Match award and the bottle of champagne that goes with it.

Because the game was 'live' on TV, and perhaps because of my televised performances against Everton, I started getting fan mail from people all over the country. They were telling me the match with Villa was the best game they had seen that season and were praising me for my brave score at the end.

It also attracted the national Press, who don't often notice unfashionable sides like 'Boro. The Sunday Mirror came to see me in the wake of those big games and Bill Thornton wrote a gushing piece about this 'find' called Tony Mowbray.The article read:

'Tony Mowbray had devoted 13 of his 24 years to the cause of Middlesbrough Football Club.

'Then, television alerted the nation to an extraordinary personality.

'Dramatic, headed goals against Everton, in the F.A. Cup and last Sunday against top-of-the-table Villa merely embellished inspirational displays which have transformed 'Tony Who' into a household name.

'Proud team manager Bruce Rioch went before the cameras to describe his skipper as a 'remarkable man'. He also said he would pick Mowbray to fly to the moon with.

'Mowbray, Saltburn-born, Redcar-raised and 'Boro-bred, was 22 when selected by Rioch to lead his young side's return from the dead 18 months ago.

'Now, in Rioch's eyes, he is Captain Fantastic...a player coveted by the likes of Manchester United yet one who has tied his colours to the mast of the club he has played with since he was a kid.'

If that wasn't enough to turn a bloke's head, stories started appearing in the papers linking me with a move to either Manchester United or Glasgow Rangers.

Then former Middlesbrough manager Jack Charlton came weighing in with even headier stuff.

Jack, by that time the boss of the Irish national side, had been commentating for TV on the Villa game I mentioned. Later, he said he was impressed by the central defensive partnership of Tony Mowbray and Gary Pallister.

He added: 'Pallister is a tremendous header of the ball with more pace than Mowbray.

'Mowbray attacks the ball well. It was nice for him to score the winner on Sunday because he was caught a little out of position for Villa's goal.

'If Mowbray was Irish, he would come into the reckoning for my team. I like a solid centre half.'

Our progress through the league had been impressive and I was delighted to be named the 1988 North East Player of the Year (incidentally, ahead of Paul Gascoigne and my old mate, Pally). But again, we left it late in the day to anchor our success. Had we beaten Leicester on the last day of the season, we would have been promoted.

But we went down 2-1 at home, consigning us to the play-offs if we were to maintain any hope of completing our fairy tale return to the First Division.

Finally, all that stood between us and glamour ties against Liverpool and Manchester United, was the London club, Chelsea.

To be played over two legs, we won the first leg at Middlesbrough 2-0, but were filled with trepidation over the return match at Stamford Bridge. Even at the time, Chelsea were burdened by a terrible hooligan problem and things seemed to be going against us when they went one goal up.

The 19th minute strike had 'Made in Scotland' written all over it. Little Pat Nevin pulled the ball back for Gordon Durie, again a Ranger, to claim his 20th goal of that season.

In a terribly intimidating atmosphere, we managed to hang on to our lead. But the scenes at the final whistle were shameful and robbed us of our real moment of glory. Chelsea fans came streaming on to the pitch and stormed towards the Middlesbrough fans. The players had to run for their lives as well, denying us our lap of honour.

Only the good efforts of the Police prevented a blood bath that day; they just managed to draw a line between the opposing sets of supporters.

We did go out, half an hour later once the Chelsea fans had dispersed, to take the acclaim of our loyal supporters. I walked to the front of the terracing to shake hands with as many of the 7,000 Middlesbrough fans as I possibly could and then threw my famous No.4 jersey into the crowd.

Despite the chaos of that day – over 100 people were arrested – the Chelsea fans could not take away the achievement of Bruce Rioch.

He had taken a bankrupt club from the depths of the Third Division to the heights of the First Division in the space of two years.

Sure, he was a real disciplinarian. His father was a Scottish regimental sergeant major and he had very fixed ideas of the way a club should be run.

But he gave us back our respect. And thanks to his leadership, the season of 1988-89 would be spent on a tour of places like Anfield and Old Trafford.

Chapter Three
Celtic and the Loneliness of the Long-distance Defender

IF I will always remember the day I agreed to sign for Celtic, there is every possibility that manager Liam Brady will recall it too. The night of 6 November 1991 and Liam and I have just concluded signing talks at Glasgow's Albany Hotel.

He gets in his car and is promptly charged by the police for drink-driving. He can't blame me. I don't drink alcohol and he certainly wasn't drinking in my company.

But it was an unfortunate end to one of the most amazing days of my life. Middlesbrough were going well at the time; in fact, they were sitting at the top of the Second Division.

There was a certain appeal to playing for, say, 17 years for the one club, hopefully then going on to be a coach, then a manager and possibly having a job with the one side for the rest of your life.

But I felt I had gone as far as I could at the club and I just thought: 'Here we go again....another season at Middlesbrough.'

I found myself feeling that I was just playing another game.....going to training.....playing another game. Training was becoming harder and harder for me to enjoy. To be honest, it was becoming hard work even to turn up at the training ground. I seemed to have lost all my motivation.

Yet if there was anything inside driving me on, it was driving me on to go elsewhere. I wanted to achieve something in the game and it rankled with me that I had been at Ayresome Park 10 years and had no winners' medals to show for it.

The closest I had come to one was when Middlesbrough battled through to the final of the Zenith Data Systems Cup in 1990.

Incredibly, I suffered a pelvic injury shortly before the final, which ruled me out of the squad. Thirty-five thousand fans were travelling down from the Northeast.

I had hardly missed a game for Middlesbrough in 10 years and now, on the only occasion the club has ever played at Wembley, I have to miss out through injury.

Everyone was gutted for me; and the manager did me the honour of asking me to lead out the team at the national stadium.

But we lost 1-0 to Chelsea and it only served to stir the deep dissatisfaction I was beginning to experience at Ayresome Park.

I had been with this club at its very lowest point, had battled with everyone else to get to the ground where every English boy dreams of playing and yet I had been denied a part in what could have been our finest hour. Maybe, I thought, Middlesbrough was not for me.

I think the new manager Lennie Lawrence could detect my discontent because he called me into his office one day in November 1991 to discuss my new contract.

I told him I needed a fresh challenge; I needed to move on....get away. I made it clear that if I was moving, I would only be prepared to go to a top five Premiership club or, dare I say it, Celtic or Rangers up here. I didn't know the first thing about Scottish football or religious affiliations so I didn't owe my allegiance to either side of the Glasgow divide.

The very next day, the manager called me up and said: 'Celtic are on the phone. Do you want to speak to Liam Brady?'

Liam seemed a nice guy on the phone so I agreed to travel up to watch Celtic's game with Neuchatel Xamax in the second round of the UEFA Cup, to see if I got a feel for the place.

I knew so little about Scotland and Glasgow that Celtic's chief scout John Kelman had to meet me at the Hamilton motorway services to show me the road to Parkhead.

There was a great atmosphere in the ground that night, with

26,000 Celtic fans urging their team to overturn a 5-1 thrashing in Switzerland a fortnight earlier.

I sneaked into the directors' box just after the kick-off to avoid being noticed. I was just in time to see Charlie Nicholas miss a penalty kick, a failure the team never really got over and they won just 1-0 on the night.

But I had been won over by the passion of the Celtic support; before the game, they were actually convinced their team could overcome that huge deficit. Liam and I went back to the Albany for that fateful, but totally drink-free, meeting.

I officially put pen to paper on November 7, the same day that Celtic announced a £10m sponsorship deal with kit manufacturers, Umbro. Everything seemed to be operating on a much higher scale than I had known before.

Anthony Vickers, a sports journalist with the Middlesbrough Evening Gazette, bade me farewell from the north east with these kind words:

'Tony Mowbray is the local boy who played his heart out for the team he loved.

'Now he is a Celtic player, but to the Ayresome Park faithful he will always be identified with Middlesbrough Football Club.

'In a turbulent decade that saw Middlesbrough fall from the heights of Division One to the brink of liquidation, Tony was the Boro.

'He was a rock at the centre of the Middlesbrough defence, leading by example and never wavering in his dedication to the side.

'Then he led the club in the fightback that saw them play their way back into the top flight, driving on a young team and firing them up in the cause.

'He was Bruce Rioch's right-hand man in a regime that put pride back in the Boro.

'Ironically, like Rioch, he was cruelly denied a role in the club's finest hour. When the Boro got to Wembley in the Zenith Data Systems Cup, he was sidelined by a serious pelvic injury while Rioch was axed before the trip to the Twin Towers.

'Now, after a decade of loyal service, he will be turning out for Celtic and no-one will begrudge him his chance to perform on a different stage.

'Tony Mowbray will be leaving Ayresome Park with a lot of memories. And he will leave behind a lot of friends.'

In my new city of Glasgow, however, it took me no time at all to discover that I had not just joined a football team, but had taken sides in a city rivalry stretching back a hundred years or maybe more.

It may be the ultimate blasphemy if you're a Celtic player but I'll say it anyway: Had it been Walter Smith, rather than Liam Brady who put in a bid for me in 1991, I would have had no hesitation in pulling on the blue jersey.

I was proud as punch with the two new Versace jackets I had bought with some of my signing-on fee.

Yet, as I walked up to Parkhead for one of my first games for the club, I realised that I had made a costly error.

'Here, what's that you've got on?,' demanded one fan as I made my way to the front door. 'What's that you're wearing?' asked the doorman as he let me in. 'What kind of jacket is that to wear here?' said the Celtic hospitality girl waiting in the foyer.

MY ROYAL BLUE VERSACE JACKET HAD CAUSED SOMETHING OF A STIR!

Howls of derision met me as I entered the dressing room. Peter Grant suggested I might get an interview for the doorman at Ibrox. All I needed, he joked, was the Rangers crest on my pocket. And physio Jimmy Steele, fresh from giving one of the players a rub-down, was being encouraged to smear his hands all over my fresh clobber.

I got the message. The jacket was never worn again, at least not in Glasgow. And it had cost me a packet.

But I was in the middle of an adventure. On my departure from the Northeast of England, I had decided not to carry north the baggage of my superstitions.

No more, would I insist on the No.4 jersey (probably someone at Parkhead would have something to say about it if I did). No more would I insist on bacon butties before a match. No, I was making a clean break and I would leave behind those ridiculous beliefs that had weighed me down for so long.

In any case, what need had I of luck? I was being feted by a club, famed throughout Europe for its pedigree of quality football. As Celtic's new £1m defender, the club were determined to give me the five-star treatment in Glasgow until I found a home of my own.

They put me up in the Albany Hotel (actually I think it had just been renamed The Forte Crest) and, of course, everything was on account.

Gary Gillespie was still in the hotel as well and I quickly found out he fancies himself as something of a gourmet. I could only watch in admiration as he ordered up all these posh dishes I had never even heard of.

The other players in the team were really good as well, trying their best to make their new arrival welcome in a strange town. John Collins invited me out to his house a couple of times for meals; there were a few nights out in Glasgow with some of the other lads, like Peter Grant.

But then, after a month, it all stopped. The novelty of living in a fancy hotel quickly wore off and I came up against the terrible problem of afternoon boredom which I know affects a lot of players living away from home.

There's so much spare time when you are a footballer – people don't realise. While Glasgow's city centre has a lot of shops, I had seen them all within the first two weeks of coming up here.

My new team-mates were great for the first month but

they've got to get on with their lives as well. They've all got families....there were hardly any single lads in the first team squad at that time. Players who have subsequently made the step up from the reserves, like Brian O'Neil and Mark McNally were unattached but there's this unwritten code which prevents reserves mixing socially with the top team. Sadly, they would not have dared to ask me out to a night-club.

To make matters worse, I suffered a serious injury in a game against Hearts within 10 days of my arrival at Celtic, when I ruptured my Achilles. This not only meant I was unable to train but I could hardly walk any distance without suffering a lot of pain as well.

So there I was, getting up in the morning and fighting through the Glasgow traffic to get to Celtic Park. While all the other lads headed off to the training ground, I was either stretched out on the treatment table or working with weights to get my strength back.

After that, as everyone else heads back to their wife and kids, you go back to the hotel and say: 'Christ, what am I going to do?'

I got into a rut of going into my room, closing the curtains and just lying down on the bed. I was bored, I was lonely and I was desperately, desperately homesick.

I was beginning to question my decision to leave my superstitions behind in England. Nothing, but nothing had gone right for me since I crossed the border.

For the first time since I was a teenager, I was on my own and I didn't like it one bit. All I had to look forward to was my evening meal at around six o'clock. And it went on like that for an agonising eight months.

Even when I was over my injury and back in the side, I would get out of Glasgow every day that I could. On days off, I would literally drive 200 miles down to Middlesbrough just to be back within my own family, my own community.

I must have put 70,000 miles on my car in that first year but there was no way I was going to stare at the four walls of a hotel if I could possibly avoid it.

I would train at Celtic on a Tuesday and as soon as I was showered and changed, I was heading back home down the M74.

I would stay until Wednesday night, then drive back to Scotland so that I'd be there for training on a Thursday morning.

Most of the time I wouldn't even be going out in Middlesbrough.

I would be quite happy in the house, just knowing that there was someone in my life sitting in the next room; that someone was there. You did not feel lonely then. Even if they were upstairs, there was somebody there.

To further complicate things, my departure from Middlesbrough co-incided with the end of a long-standing relationship; Nicola and I had been going out for six or seven years and we had become engaged.

But after living together, we had come to realise that we were not compatible. If you don't know you want to make the commitment after five or six years, then it's not meant to be, is it?

Nicky went to London to get away from the goldfish bowl atmosphere of Middlesbrough. After all, she had been the girlfriend of the club captain for all those years; she felt enormous pressure with people wondering what she was going to do with her life. At home, she felt she couldn't go anywhere or do anything without people pointing her out.

But even though we both knew it wasn't going to happen for us, our separation and loneliness meant that we were still regularly talking to each other on the phone.

Bored out of my head, I would get into my room and call her up, ask how she was getting on at work – you know the daft things people talk about.

We didn't realise it, but we were artificially keeping alive something that should have been laid to rest. We were both scared to make that final cut-off, and with me being so lonely in Glasgow, I desperately wanted to keep hold of something that reminded me of home.

I honestly don't know what football clubs can do about that sort of problem. It does seem daft to spend £1m on a player and then allow him to grow unhappy and discontented.....but what is the alternative?

Big football clubs in England have a history of putting their young players in digs, an ordinary home with an ordinary family where there's less chance of them becoming homesick.

Wise as I find that policy to be, I can hardly see a club like Celtic telling their new £1m player that he's going to be living with a landlady!

Yet maybe if I knew then what I know now, I might just have taken them up on the offer.

It could be that Tommy Burns is initiating a new policy or perhaps it's just that he reckons I might be in need of the company right now, but he suggested that I put up the club's new signing, Pierre van Hooijdonk, at my home in Bothwell.

In the end, we decided against it but I still think in principle, it's a good idea not to leave a lad to his own devices in a strange town. I could have given Pierre a grounding in what Glasgow means; given him someone to drive him around Glasgow and show him what's what.

It's a luxury that simply wasn't open to me when I first came to the club.

Chapter Four
Magic – a Girl Called Bernadette

EVERYONE knows footballers are a posey breed; haunting night-clubs in their designer gear and chatting up every woman in the place. Not me.

You're more likely to find me sitting in a corner, having a quiet natter with someone I like, rather than trying to make an impression on an assembled gathering.

And that's where I was the night I was introduced to a young dark-haired girl called Bernadette Doyle. It was Victoria's Night-club in Glasgow's Sauchiehall Street and I had gone along after a Wednesday night match with some of my team-mates.

Wednesday nights had become something of an institution with the players. We would all meet up at Charlie Nicholas's pub, Cafe Cini, and head up to Victoria's after having had a few drinks.

There's a place called The Piano Bar at the very top of the building. There's no loud music in there; it's a place to go if you want to talk.

Peter Grant knew Bernadette because her sister, Mary, is married to Willie McStay, brother of Celtic's captain, Paul.

I can't remember what my opening line to her was...it was probably pathetic. But what I do remember is that I dazzled her with magic.

Since arriving at the club, I think I had shown my matches trick to everyone even remotely connected with Celtic. You do it with a book of matches and it's one of those tricks where people reckon they know how it's done . . . but come back 15 minutes later and ask you to do it again.

Anyway, it probably broke the ice between us and we went on

to talk until about three in the morning. Or, rather, I did.

Bernadette just sat and listened, as I poured out my heart about the girl I had left behind and how I was pretty lonely in my new house in Bothwell.

Looking back, I think I captivated her without really intending to; here was a footballer who was not trying to chat her up; who was being sincere about the only girl he had really ever been serious about. And when I stood up and just said: 'Night, night' I think you could have knocked her down with a feather.

She later explained any other guy in a Glasgow night-club would have tried to take her home or walk her to the taxi. But I had just left it at that and got my coat. She was stunned.

Maybe that had an effect on her. Maybe she started wondering: 'Well, what's he all about, then?'

In any case, her sister Elizabeth has said that Bernie told her she had just met someone with the same standards as her . . . someone who's honest and loyal and wasn't trying to take her home.

It was something she had never come across in her life. She was a pretty girl. I'm sure she had been chatted up hundreds of times. But the one time she wasn't chatted up was the one time she became really interested.

I'm not saying it's what she had been looking for but Liz will tell you she had never, ever met anyone who was on the same level as her. Bern was always preaching to her brothers and sisters, even her mam and dad.

If Liz had a new boyfriend, Bern would tell her: 'You're too good for him . . . I've heard he's been out with his mates while he leaves you in the house.'

Although she was the third youngest of nine children, it was Bernie who would lecture them all on who was and who wasn't good enough for them. She was almost an agony aunt to them; if anyone had a problem, it was to wise Bernie that they would turn for advice. She was the one with such high standards. And people in her own family sometimes struggled to match them.

I honestly don't know what it was that drove me to see her a second time; I can't say we got on great that first night because she hardly spoke. Maybe it was sheer boredom and I found myself, one afternoon when I had nothing to do, thinking about the dark-haired girl from the night-club.

I remembered the name of the fashion store where she worked in Paisley, so, after training one day, I took a drive over that way. I could never have walked into a shop and asked if Bernadette was in; no, I decided I'd have a casual browse around the menswear and I'd act surprised if I saw her and say something trite like 'Oh, how are you doing, I forgot you worked in here.'

She wasn't in. So I bought a bloody John Smedley black top I neither needed nor wanted.

But it wasn't long before I was back and our relationship just took off from there. You appreciate, fairly quickly, when someone is on the same wavelength as you. You can talk for hours and hours and it seems like 10 minutes.

Bernadette moved to a small clothes store in Glasgow called The Institute. Instead of driving home after training, I would head into the city and park right outside her shop.

The whole afternoon would be spent there....the two of us talking away. It was easy because it was a small shop and she didn't have a boss breathing down her neck. If a customer came in, I'd wander off to look at the shirts or something and then I'd be back chatting with Bernie.

We got on so, so well together. But although we were spending more and more time in each other's company, it was not yet a formal boyfriend/girlfriend relationship. We were almost mates at first. We had found someone to talk to and confide in.

She would say it was her lunch-time and I would casually

reply: 'Oh well, I've got nothing to do. Do you fancy going for a coffee?' For the first couple of months, she simply refused to eat in front of me.

She would ask for a coffee and it would sit in front of her, untouched. I'd ask her if she wanted a sandwich and she'd leave that as well.

We even once went out to a restaurant for a meal and she didn't order a thing...so I had to eat on my own. I still don't know what it was, but she was just too nervous to consume any food at all in my presence. Strangely enough, I thought there was something nice about being able to have that effect on someone.

I loved how naive she was about everything, how innocent. In conversation, I would pry about old boyfriends...where she'd been on holiday....what she had done with her life so far.

But she hadn't had any boyfriends. And that absolutely fascinated me. Back where I come from, girls are courting at 17, if not before. Yet here was a girl of 23 telling me she had never had a steady boyfriend. Unbelievable.

Some people will tell you that she was so innocent, she never even kissed a boy before she met me. Bernie, herself, said she may have kissed one boy but was never even comfortable with that. Amazing.

Without realising it, I was beginning to put her on a pedestal. You know you are in awe of someone when you are physically scared to touch them in case they break. She seemed so fragile.

Walking down a street, I was so awkward with her. I didn't know where to put my hand.

This was a girl who had kissed just one boy, so you weren't going to slap your hand on her backside. I was also careful not to put my hand too far around her shoulder, for fear of offending her.

Funnily enough, she was so worldly-wise in other ways. She had been the manageress of a bar at 19, with a staff of 10 sreporting to her. So when we were on a night out, Bernie seemed to know half of Glasgow. She would point to someone and tell me that was Tommy, who used to take the empties out the back. Or she would wave to someone else, then whisper to me:'I had to sack him once.....'

Everyone wanted to hug Bernie. At first, I didn't like it when blokes cuddled her but then I realised that was Bernie's way with everyone.

A whole new world was opening up to me. Coming from a place like Middlesbrough, well, you've just got your mates. But, thanks to Bernie, my life was beginning to blossom.

Entire avenues appeared from nowhere. If I wanted joinery work doing, then Joe Bloggs down the road would help me out; if I needed carpets for the house, Sammy would see me all right.

It was such an exciting time. And when our relationship developed into the full boyfriend/girlfriend thing, she positively glowed when we were out.

In turn, she revelled in the new circle of friends that I was able to introduce her to. It was probably a circle she had seen operating before because of her family's links with Celtic....maybe she had been looking on from the sidelines but never felt a part of.

But now she was feeling she belonged to the club . Now Charlie Nicholas was calling her 'my girl' and she loved it. Charlie is a very street-wise guy and he knows the girls who have been about and he knows the ones who have taken a pride in themselves. He knew what a class act she was.

It took her to a different level than she had been at before. She was bubbling...so effervescent. She was like a bundle of energy, ready to explode on a night out.

If she was proud of me, then suddenly I had become settled and contented with my life.

It was hard to reconcile this new, colourful city with the place

I had only ever seen before through the windows of a lonely hotel bedroom.

And it was all thanks to Bernie.

Chapter Five
Board Games at Celtic Park

IT'S ONLY by looking back now that I realise I was an unwitting pawn in the great game of chess that finally ended in check-mate for the White and Kelly families, who had run Celtic for generations.

In November 1991, when I signed for the Hoops, the now-legendary discontent of the Celtic support was already bubbling away.

The club had not won anything since the 1989 Scottish Cup Final, when wee Joe Miller's strike dumped Rangers 1-0 in what is widely recognised as one of the dullest finals in the history of the competition.

And just weeks before I signed on the dotted line, Celtic had endured a punishing three days by being beaten 2-0 in the league by Rangers and then sent crashing out of the Skol Cup by Premier League strugglers Airdrie. To cap the fans' frustration, Liam told the after-match press conference at Broomfield that his team 'had nothing to be ashamed of'. I know that comment upset a great many Celtic supporters.

This, of course, was a state of affairs entirely new to Celtic's following, brought up on a mouth-watering diet of triumph on the domestic and European front.

The year before their last trophy victory, there had been the euphoria of the 1988 League and Cup double. And then there's the small matter of nine league flags in a row during the Jock Stein era. But Celtic's failure to win honours in the 1990s also co-incided with an incredibly-successful run for Rangers, so this new situation was even more painful for Celtic fans to swallow.

I now believe that in 1991, the Celtic board gave in to the growing belief that their big problem could only be solved by throwing money at it. Liam Brady, appointed manager in June that year, was perhaps the start of their new approach. By signing an internationally renowned figure like Liam, and presumably paying him a wage commensurate with his status, Celtic would, in theory, be able to tap into a wealth of knowledge gleaned in England and Italy.

He was given the go-ahead to raid the infamous Celtic biscuit tin, to splash out on players from whatever league in much the same way as Graeme Souness had been allowed to do at Rangers, five years earlier.

Perhaps Celtic fans now shudder at the investments Liam made with his new-found wealth, names like Gary Gillespie, Tony Mowbray and, dare I say it, Tony Cascarino.

We were the Millionaire Club, all of us costing Celtic transfer fees in at least seven figures. Yet the impact made by any one of us could hardly be described as awe-inspiring.

Measured against the task for which he was bought, Tony Cascarino had a disastrous time at Celtic Park. His inability to stick the ball in the net is now the stuff of legend....but did it get him down? If it did, it certainly never showed.

To see Tony in the dressing room, you would never believe he was a player under pressure. In fact, he had such an easy-going personality he was able to laugh at his own dismal goal-scoring record.

Amazing as it may seem, he had an unshakeable belief in his own ability; he knew what his strengths were. Believe me, as a defender, one of the last guys you want to see running on to a cross in the box is Tony Cascarino. I have played against him at Millwall and I can assure you he's a real handful, a great big attacker with fantastic body strength and excellent heading ability.

I am not joking when I compare him to Mark Hateley, the big front man who has had a phenomenal strike rate with Rangers.

The difference between the two players is the team in which

they played; Rangers players know that if they manage to get high balls into the penalty box, there is every chance that Mark Hateley will get on the end of them.

The same goes for Tony Cascarino. Played properly at Celtic Park, this big Irish internationalist would have been good for 20 goals a season. I know that for sure, because he produced that sort of return year-in and year-out for Millwall.

People might sneer at that remark and say 'Well, that's only the English First Division', but from experience, I know that it's no mug's game down there.

If you were to take out Celtic and Rangers from Scotland's top division, the premier league up here is inferior to the English First Division.

At Celtic, Tony Cascarino was trapped in a team which would pass five-yard balls along the ground. That was not playing to Tony's strength, so no-one should be surprised that he used to fall over his own boot-laces.

But if Liam Brady had used a winger to sling some decent crosses onto Tony's head, I am sure he would have been stuffing them away in the net with monotonous regularity.I had a lot of soul-searching chats with him about his role in the team. He knew he didn't look good on the park. But then he had never been trained for the silky style of soccer which Liam seemed to be imposing on the side. Paul McStay was slipping one-two's to Tony's feet but this style of football was totally alien to him. Quite simply, Tony was an up-and-at-'em attacker of the old school and he ended up confused as to why Liam bought him in the first place. As soon as he saw Celtic's style of play, he knew he'd be the fall-guy.

Back in the dressing room, however, Tony would pick up a newspaper which maybe had slaughtered him for a performance . . . and he'd make a joke out of it. He was a really likeable guy who never had a fixed-odds coupon out of his hand.

And I remember recently seeing an article in the Sunday Mail about how the French are raving about this new signing for Marseilles who's knocking 'em in good-style. Tony Cascarino.

He was posing with a glass of champagne and a fat cigar on a picturesque hillside on the Cote d'Azur. So who do you think had the last laugh?

But while in Scotland, Cas was only one of the three Brady buys which were coming in for stick from the Press.

They were lumping me, Cas and Gillie altogether as million-pound flops. Gary could look unbelievable on a fine, sunny day at Parkhead. Had he moved to Manchester United, for example, I'm sure he would have glided along for a couple of seasons on the smooth Old Trafford surface.

And that's the thing about Gillie....he moved so effortlessly you thought he was on rollers.

But take him to Brockville on a soaking-wet Wednesday night, with a pitch as heavy as treacle, and he's really not the player you would want beside you.

As for me, bad injuries in my early days at Parkhead must have left Liam thinking he'd been sold a crock. It wasn't my fault, but I suppose I was a 'flop' in the sense that Celtic had spent £1 million on me and here was I, unable to show what I could do. So without doubt, I contributed to the pressure which was already building on the manager.

The funny thing to remember in all of this is that Celtic's fortunes directly depended on what was going on out there on the park. If we had been winning everything out of sight, questions would simply not have been asked of the board.

But I remember walking down the street in Glasgow and fans stopping me to demand what had happened to all of the gate receipts taken in during the fabulously successful spells in the 1960s and 1970s.

How was I to know what had happened to them? I was still at school! But the very fact that I was being asked such up-front questions reflected the fact that discontent with Celtic Football

Club had now become deep-seated.

In August 1992, in the parlance of the football sports writer, Liam mounted a 'raid' on the south by busting Celtic's record transfer fee. He paid West Ham £1.5 million for their attacking mid fielder, Stuart Slater.

Sadly, it would be four months before the 23-year-old England 'B' internationalist was to find the net.

It turned out that the strike against Aberdeen on 2 December was to be his first goal in 76 games for either the Hammers or Celtic. And he would only go on to score one more before the end of the season.

Stuart's one of the most down-to-earth guys you could meet in football. He's just a quiet, well-spoken young man who loves playing the game; hardly the type of bloke you would want to burden with the title 'Celtic's most expensive footballer'.

These were not the shoulders on which to thrust the hopes and aspirations of Celtic supporters, starved of honours for three years now.

Stuart had played all of his football in London. His transfer to Celtic had been something of a whirlwind affair, with Stuart only told of Liam Brady's interest in a 10-second telephone call from Hammers manager, Billy Bonds.

Londoners are notorious for coming into clubs and trying to take over the dressing room. It would be fair to say Stuart never tried that. He was really, really quiet. So when the stick started to fly and people were critical of him, he just didn't have the depth of character to get him through it. He was transferred to Ipswich for half his original transfer fee only 13 months after he walked through the Parkhead doors.

If the so-called 'star' players I have mentioned were disappointed at the path their Celtic careers were taking and the supporters were feeling as though they were in some way cheated, just think how the Celtic board must have felt.

They had broken with their traditional frugal approach to

transfer fees, players at the club were earning money previous Celtic players could only have dreamed of, and yet we were locked in our least successful spell for generations. Their grand plan of holding on to power through a 'spend, spend, spend' policy was crumbling before their very eyes. It might be a further three years before they would finally lose control of the club, but I am convinced the seeds of their downfall were sown in 1991.

As a player, I never really had any contact with the men who ran Celtic then. We look upon directors as the guys who come whizzing into the club car park in their Mercedes on match days and go walking upstairs for drinkies in the boardroom before kick-off.

I think the closest I ever got to any of them was before my testimonial game with my old club, Middlesbrough, when the chairman, Kevin Kelly, presented me with a nice crystal memento from the club.

But if his statement to me was brief on that occasion, his comments to an increasingly hostile Press were becoming not just briefer but fewer and fewer.

The Press were jacking up the pressure on Celtic every day. I don't know whether they realise it or not, but the influence held by a few newspapers in Scotland is so unbelievably powerful.

They not only influence the three million-or-so people who read their articles every day, they exert enormous influence on players as well.Any footballer who tells you he isn't stung by criticism in a match report is spinning you a line. We read the papers, like everyone else. Of course, it hurts. No-one likes to be told they are useless at whatever they are being paid to do, be it a joiner, a bus driver or a football player.

I know it hurts me. But what was going on in the Press in 1992 onwards was different. Celtic have always stood accused of 'paranoia' whenever they point to unfair treatment by the Press. Well, I have no axe to grind either way but even I can see that

Celtic do not receive a fair crack of the whip from the Scottish media.

Whether it's because the club used to be great and sports editors feel we should be great again, I don't know. But, for example, you would pick up a paper and read how you had lost in the semi-final of a cup. For most other clubs in Scotland, that would have been the end of it.

But this was Celtic and the sports pages would drive home the message in big type that this marked FOUR YEARS of failing to win a trophy; the next year it would be FIVE TROPHYLESS YEARS and so the screw on us was turned.

The biased coverage affected the supporters because they had to go in to work that day, knowing that Tam Broon, the bloke he worked beside who supported Rangers, had probably read the same article.

But it affected the playing staff at Celtic as well. I couldn't put my finger on it and say that, one day, I walked into the dressing room and realised that the pressure had descended on us right there and then; it was a gradual thing which built and built and built until it came to a climax.

We were losing big, big games at bad, bad times. In my first season at Celtic, we lost 1-0 to Rangers in the semi-final of the Scottish Cup; the following year we lost to them again by the same score in the semi-final of the League Cup . These were big games to lose. You win those games and you go on to win the cup. People were beginning to ask if we couldn't handle the pressure.

In a way, that's a tag we still have to bury. In season 1994/95 we managed to win one of those big games, the Coca Cola Cup semi-final against Aberdeen, only to lose the final against Raith Rovers.

But we also won another, the Scottish Cup semi-final with Hibernian which gave us a crack at Airdrie in the final.

Even so, despite the pressure every one of us was under, the players still steadfastly refused to start blaming one another. Sure, there is the odd altercation after a match when various members of the team have a dig at each other but it's usually one bite then it's over in a flash. There are exceptions to that rule, of course, and they're all called Peter Grant.

He moans and whinges all the time. Granty tries to coax everybody through a game sometimes . . . 'get this' . . . 'get that' he'll bark at you. He knows he irritates people at times and that's not necessarily a bad thing. It shows he cares.

But there are many occasions when you have to tell Peter Grant: 'Hey, piss off! You look after your department and we'll look after the back. I sometimes have to tell him to concentrate on doing his job and we'll get along just fine.

Granty tries to do everybody's job on occasion and it's really only when he is in full flow that you really see individuals displaying tension or showing signs of pressure.

We could have won the last six competitions we took part in and Granty would still be bickering at people.

So it would be wrong to suggest that the Celtic home dressing room was a hot-bed of discontent with the ruling board. We were professional people, paid to do a specific job which we were not doing particularly well. But we did not see it as our place to level blame at the people at the top of the club.

Having said that, I was aware that there were a couple of factions in the dressing room who, shall we say, were more aware than others of what was going on concerning the politics of Celtic.

Most of my information about what was going on came via the newspapers. We never had any team discussions, suggesting 'Right, we're going to do this as a team' because it was our responsibility. It just never happened.

The league match with Kilmarnock on 1 March 1994 was meant to mark a turning point in the attitude of the Celtic supporters towards the board. A pressure group, Celts for

Change, had called for a boycott of the game, to show for good just how deep-rooted the fans' disaffection with the club had become.

We hadn't been getting particularly good crowds at Celtic Park for a while before the game. Still, I think 10,000 fans turned up.

All I remember is people wearing white T-shirts with letters on them, spelling out 'Support The Team. Sack The Board'.

Players would have to be really tough individuals to claim that events like that do not affect them. This season, playing our games at Hampden Park, we have discovered to our cost how the lack of an encouraging atmosphere can be measured in the number of points dropped at the end of a season.

Having a good support behind you is so vital for concentration and motivation. I have played games with Middlesbrough when we've been ordered to harness that extra player on the terracings.

In some 'away' games, we would go out to stifle the opposition in the first 20 minutes. After that time, the 'home' fans will start getting frustrated and they'll take out that frustration on their own team. Then the players get edgy and some of them will stop looking for the ball so much.

That's why we found ourselves in a vicious circle during the major protests against the board.

Fans wanted success, it's true. But are they likely to get success on the park, where it matters, if they spend their time chanting 'Sack the Board' rather than 'You'll Never Walk Alone'?Celtic fans were in a really funny mood at that time. Did they want their team to win matches? Or would victory only win more breathing space for the beleaguered-looking board?

Players need to hear the roar of their fans. They need that burst of noise after you win a corner and the rising vocal expectation that a goal is coming up.

I am sure that, like the Press, supporters do not realise the power they wield on a Saturday. Players do sit down after a game and remark: 'God, did you hear the noise from the fans today! It was fantastic.'

On such a day, 9 November 1991, I made my debut for Celtic. It was a home league game against Aberdeen at Celtic Park and thirty-seven thousand people thought it a sufficiently attractive fixture to hand over their hard-earned cash at the turnstile.

The atmosphere was electric, I'll never forget it. This was probably the biggest crowd I had ever played in front of. I recall The Jungle, Celtic's famous standing terraces facing the main stand, as a sea of faces singing songs I had never heard before. At Middlesbrough, the crowd would congregate behind either goal, but here they were massed all around the ground. Fantastic.

I was at a supporter's club dinner in Livingston recently, when a fan reminded me of the game and how he had taken out a bet at 33-1 that Tony Mowbray would be the first scorer of the match.

I very nearly made him rich, and from 35 yards out at that. The ball was played across, square, to me and after a little touch, it just sat up for me. It was one of those balls you catch sweetly, really sweetly and I was sure it was heading for the top corner. It changed direction slightly in the air and crashed on to the underside of the bar.

The place just went crazy. They launched into singing my name. I loved it, but then I thought: 'Christ, I hope they don't expect that every week!'

I had only scored one goal in my life from that distance: it was for Middlesbrough against Norwich, the first goal we scored after returning to the First Division. And the next time I (nearly) do it is on my debut for Celtic! If that had gone in the net, people would probably have allowed me to play poorly for the rest of the season but wouldn't breathe a word of criticism because of that one cracking goal against Aberdeen. In any case, we won

2-1 with goals from Charlie Nicholas and Gerry Creaney.

4 March 1994 signalled a fresh start for Celtic Football Club. The old board, which had clung on to power under such hostile attack, finally slipped down the abyss to be replaced by new chief executive, the Scots-Canadian Fergus McCann. We thought the new management team also included Brian Dempsey, because I remember watching him on TV that wet night, standing on the steps of Celtic Park declaring: 'The battle is over; the rebels have won!'

But he faded from the picture very quickly, leaving Fergus to re-shape the club in his likeness.

He is a very interesting character, is Fergus. It's obvious he has finely-tuned motivational qualities in his make-up because he has imparted these to us on occasion in the dressing room. He came in before our first game under his control, the league game with St Johnstone at McDiarmid Park. He just told us to remember that we were playing for Celtic, a special club, and urged us on to 'get out there and do it'. We did it, by just one goal to nil.

Whether that type of thing is right for the dressing room, I don't know. Football players can be funny sometimes with non-footballing people but he was simply telling us that each one of us would be given a chance to shine under the new regime.

He still pops his head round the door on occasion but it's clear that he knows it's not really his place.

He knows his place is in the suites of offices at Celtic Park and in the boardroom, looking after the investment of £9 million which he put into the club.

I am no wiser than anyone else about just how bad the finances of Celtic were allowed to become under the old board; I read the papers just like anyone else so, by all accounts, they were in a shocking state.

A few more hours, and the Bank of Scotland were prepared to put this great institution into the hands of the Receiver.

To someone who had already been through that scenario at Middlesbrough, it would have been a horrendous coincidence if the only other club in my entire career went the same way.

After all, few players in this country have had to face the liquidation of one club, never mind two.

But I don't think any of the players ever believed bankruptcy would be allowed to happen. We knew there were these people, waiting in the wings, desperate to inject large amounts of money into the club.

And we knew that Celtic was always going to be a sound business proposition because of the huge reservoir of support waiting for the right moment to flood through the gates.

Fergus is a tough businessman and I believe you can only run the finances of a football club along very tough principles.

He knows exactly where he is going and because of that single-minded determination, you can already see the signs that the club has started to turn the corner.

He moved very quickly to ditch the old dream of re-locating to a stadium at Cambuslang, preferring to upgrade Celtic Park, the 'Paradise' that enjoys a special place in the hearts of Celtic supporters everywhere; with us due to be back there for the start of the 1995/96 season, few people could have galvanised all of the necessary authorities so quickly.

But I honestly don't know what to expect when we return to the all-seated Celtic Park after the huge ground changes that have taken place there. The Jungle has gone, of course, to be replaced by a monster of a stand which can accommodate 26,000 supporters.

The potential support of Celtic is such that if we win the Scottish Cup in May, there is no reason why we can't get 60,000 people to turn up and back us again.

As Greavsie used to say, 'football's a funny old game' and it's amazing just how quickly a club's fortunes can turn around.

Just look at Newcastle United. They endured a similar

boardroom battle in 1991 at a time when they were attracting crowds of less than 10,000. Newcastle were bottom of the Second Division and it was well-publicised that if they dropped into the Third Division, the club would not have been able to service its debt. They would have gone bust.

The so-called 'outsiders' led by Sir John Hall won control of the club – and now look at them. They have offered a serious challenge to Blackburn Rovers and Manchester United this season and they even get 3000 people turning up to watch them train.

From a situation where just four years ago hardly anyone was interested in them, Newcastle have a 40,000-capacity stadium that's still not big enough for the number of people who want to see them play.

The very same thing can happen at Celtic. I had a gaze at the new stand the other day from the directors' box and it looks out of this world. We're desperate to experience the wall of noise which should come from it when we run out for the start of the new season.

But I can't help thinking back to the reception I got from The Jungle on my debut and I just think it's a shame that we still can't have a certain part of the ground where standing is allowed, as long as there are strict controls on the number of people going in.

A standing terracing suits the kind of supporter who likes teaming up with all his mates but it also suits the guy who goes on his own. If he doesn't like the fact that the bloke beside him is shouting obscenities, he can simply shift away to another part of the terracing.

And I honestly believe that part of the reason for the quiet atmosphere at Hampden this year is down to the fact that all the fans are seated...and many are seated next to people they have never met before and are perhaps too embarrassed to shout out in their presence.

Winning a trophy with Celtic has become extremely

important to me; it's the reason I came to the club in the first place. You only have to walk through the corridors at Parkhead, to see the walls adorned with old trophies and pennants from foreign sides, to appreciate the club's illustrious pedigree.

There are numerous mementoes of glory games against footballing giants like Real Madrid, Inter Milan and Manchester United.

Well, in a Scottish context, I am now with a side like Manchester United and I see a winner's medal as a reward for the effort I have put into my game during my career.

I have to admit, perhaps after a defeat by Partick Thistle, to harbouring the idea that it would be great to return to English football. The game has mushroomed out of all proportion to the set-up I left in 1991.

The advent of live TV coverage and the Premiership has created an altogether more glamorous occasion, even for ordinary league games.

Stadia have been transformed through the much-needed investment of millions of pounds.

I have got Sky at home and I have to marvel at the build-up an average match like Ipswich and Norwich gets on the box. It's an event.

I am 32 next birthday and I would hate to think that I would go all the way through professional football without at least one major honour to show for it.

Sure, Celtic's status has slipped in recent years but I still consider us among the Top Two teams in Scotland. The managers of other teams, like Motherwell, Hibs, Hearts or Aberdeen occasionally engage in undisguised kidology by claiming to be a greater force in the game than us. But when you look at the support Celtic enjoyed in the two Scottish Cup semi-final ties this year against Hibs, you know this is a giant just beginning to wake up.

Ten years ago, there would not have been any doubt about

who the top two clubs in Scotland were; our gaffer Tommy Burns is forever reminding us that standards have slipped. But I know, only too well, that there are several other players as well as me at Celtic who badly need to win something. And soon.

Chapter Six
The Rocky Road to Romance

THE call which led to me breaking up with my new girlfriend Bernadette Doyle came while I was driving her to my home one night. It was Nicola, my old fiancee from down south, calling me on my car phone.

She was offering what I had only been dreaming of; she would come up to visit me in Scotland to see if there was still anything left between us.

It was one of the biggest decisions of my life. I had found this bubbly, energetic girl who had opened up all of my horizons in Scotland. She loved going out with me. We had tremendous fun every time we met and we had started to move in a great, new circle of friends. And yet I'm having to say to her one day: 'Look, we're going to have to stop this.'

I didn't want us to split up but I had been going on about this girl for two years, phoning her from time to time, never really able to get her out of my mind. Bernie knew how besotted I had been about Nicola, and indeed it was by talking about my old girlfriend that I had captured Bernie's attention in the first place.

She had even been in the car, maybe I was taking her home from work or something, and the phone would ring. Nicky. There was always this terrible atmosphere when that happened.

With some justification, Bernie must have been thinking: 'Christ, it's that Nicola again from down south. Where does that leave me?'

It was February, 1993. Bernie and I had been going out for just over three months. By my warped way of thinking, I calculated that it would be easier to tell Bernie, rather than turn down Nicola, whom I had known for years.

I just thought that if I did not take the chance with Nicola, I might never know if we were meant to be.

Trying to break it to Bernie was not easy. Let's just say she took it rather badly.

But what was I doing? Things were going so well. We were made for each other. We could talk and talk for hours about nothing and everything.

And here's me, the biggest prat on earth, telling her I am choosing another girl over her. I can't stress too much how devastated I was about having to do that. But it was almost like I needed to perform an exorcism; invite in the spirit that had been haunting me and then send it on its way.

Anyway, I managed to upset Bernadette so much that she fled the country. She went to stay a fortnight at her sister Mary's house in Ireland. Mary's husband, Willie, was then manager of Sligo Rovers.

Back in Scotland, Nicky had driven up to stay with me. But I knew within two days that it was not going to work out. I am a very jealous person and the little green-eyed monster was eating away at me; I wanted to know what she had been doing, and who with.

She got up one morning and said: 'I thing we both know, don't we?' And she just got into her car and went.

I got a phone number for Willie and Mary's house and tried to explain to Bernie what had happened. I called her up at two in the morning. We were still talking at 5.30 a.m. How do you speak to someone for nearly four hours in the middle of the night?

By coincidence, Celtic were due to fly to Dublin on 3 March for a series of games against Irish teams. I found out that Willie was driving from Sligo to come to one of the matches, I think it was against Shelbourne, to see Paul play. I was sure he'd bring Bernadette with him – when I saw him come to the door of the hotel and Bernie wasn't there, I was gutted.

I went straight upstairs and phoned Bernie in Sligo from my room. She said: 'I didn't want to embarrass you in front of all the other players by coming to the hotel.'

So I had to wait until I got back to Scotland, after the tour finished four or five days later, to try to make my peace with her.

Our first meeting on my return was not icy, but it was uncomfortable. I jumped into the car and drove to see her in the shop. I think I had hurt her so much, she wasn't about to dive straight back into my arms, forgive me and tell me I was the greatest guy in the world.

When something like that happens, you have to build bridges again. I realised that I had kicked her in the teeth. I would have to regain her trust and I knew that would not happen overnight.

But by the end of that year, we were very much an item. We were spending every second of every spare minute of every day together. It was a very intense, loving, caring relationship where we both couldn't bear to be apart.

The June of 1993 saw the two of us embark on our first holiday together and with typical Mowbray efficiency, I planned our trip to Disney World and the Caribbean with almost military precision.

We stayed at The Grand Floridian, one of the world's top hotels within yards of the Magic Kingdom. To cap it all, Linda Evans from 'Dallas' was staying there at the same time and Michael Jackson checked in the week after we left.

It was an education for Bernadette. I suppose the hotel was really too pompous for her liking but I have learned, touring the world with football teams, that in these places your money is as good as anyone else's. I would tell her : 'Look, we've paid our money. We can walk into the foyer in our sand shoes if we want to.'

Back in 1988, Middlesbrough had had a fabulous trip to Canada and America, as something of a reward for our successful season. We stayed at tremendous hotels in Calgary,

Vancouver, Seattle, San Francisco and New York.

The games were very low-key because the tour came at the end rather than the start of the season. We played teams like the Calgary Kickers and the Seattle Sounders. The reason we played in Seattle was because Bruce Rioch had been with the American club towards the end of his playing career and he still knew a lot of people there.

In New York, we did all the tourist things like going up the Empire State Building and such, but I found the 18 days we were away rather tiresome.

I know it must sound nice, staying in some of the best hotels the U.S. has to offer and turning up for the occasional kick-about where nothing's really at stake.

But it had been a long, hard season for us in England and sometimes you feel like chilling out, I suppose, and just spending time with your family.

Anyway, I was much happier the next time I was in America, with Bernie.

Every day was special to us. Bernadette was accustomed to travelling because her dad's job took him all over the world. But this was her first real holiday away and I would love little things, like taking the lead in airports and telling her: 'Look darling, we need to go down this way.'

After 12 days in Florida, we headed down to Miami to meet the cruise ship *Majesty of the Seas*, the biggest liner of her type in the world.

It was the most marvellous, marvellous time of my life. We went to Jamaica, Mexico and Grand Cayman. I have these pictures of Bernadette emerging from the surf at Dunns River Falls in Jamaica. She looked like a goddess.

On board this fabulous floating hotel, you've never seen food like it. We got into a routine of an evening: it was dinner, then we went to a cabaret show and then we'd wander into the casino for half an hour, followed by a disco and the midnight buffet.

Success at my feet (above) . . . a cup-winning team at the Lakes Estate Junior School.

High flyer (below) . . . I end up the Middlesbrough jam in the sandwich with two Aston Villa players

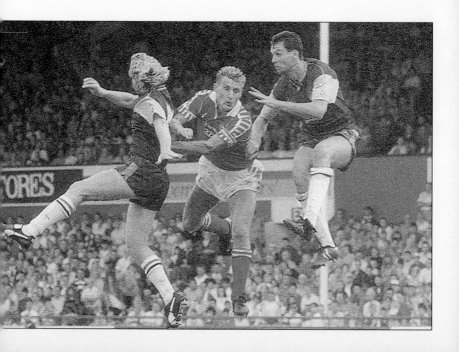

Walk on part
(above) . . . I am
privileged to lea
out the 'Boro tea
for the Zenith D
Systems Cup Fir
at Wembley

Cover story (left
. . . The
Middlesbrough
fanzine pays me
Megga Mogga
tribute on my
departure to Cel

Bye bye 'Boro (above) . . . Bidding farewell to the Middlesbrough fans at our away game at Barnsley

Heads you win (right) . . . Scoring in Celtic's 3-1 win over Dundee United on the day before my wedding

Bawl bhoy
(left) . . . I
can't help
showing my
feelings over
a strike
against
Motherwell

You cannot
be serious
(below) . . .
Referee Les
Mottram
sticks my
name in his
book

One of my favourite pictures (above) . . . Henry McInnes took this snap of me and Bernadette on our engagement

Dressed to thrill (right) . . . Bernie and I enjoy a night on board our Caribbean cruise ship, Majesty of the Seas

A face in the crowd (above) . . Bernadette waves to a friend in the Parkhead stand before a match with Motherwell

A match made in heaven (left) . . . bravery on our wedding day

A flicker of hope . . . Bernadette keeps the flame alive
during our visit to Lourdes

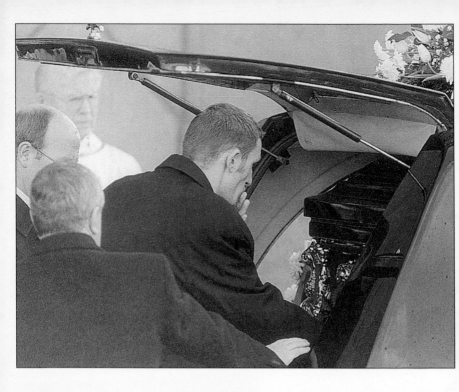

Farewell my lovely (above) . . .a fond kiss for Bernie as she leaves the church on her final journey.

Another fight begins (left) . . . A smile for the photographers as I get back down to training after Bernie's death.

After that, we might have a romantic stroll on the deck.

I remember trying to get a bit of peace at the card table one night in the casino and handing Bernadette $50 to play the fruit machines. I was sure that would keep her busy for a while because the machines accepted quarters, so she had quite a handful of change.

Two minutes later, she was back at my side. She had only won $250 with one of her first quarters . . . Proudly, she handed me a bucket, overflowing with money. 'Here,' she said, 'I want you to have this.'

I took her picture, with the bucket on her head.

Spending so much time together obviously spoiled me. Back home, I simply could not wait for Bernie to finish work. I would leave Parkhead at lunchtime after training and drive into Glasgow. I would stand and chat to her from 2 p.m. until it was time to go home.

Then I would drive her to her mum's in Barrhead, drive her to my house in Bothwell, where we would watch videos, probably eat a Chinese meal, and then drive her back home at 11 p.m. Then, of course, I would have to drive 25 miles home again, close to midnight.

The sheer physical strain of driving over 100 miles every day in the name of love sometimes made me a bit frayed at the edges.

Bernadette would reply in typically cheeky fashion about the long-distance love affairs of the McStay brothers.

She'd say: 'Willie used to do the journey for Mary . . . and never complained. Paul used to do it from Larkhall and Ann-Marie lived in GREENOCK!'

I knew she was worth it but if I was feeling a bit low and it was getting near to 11 p.m., I'd say: 'Can't you just stay tonight, darling? I'll phone your dad and tell him you'll sleep in the spare room.' But she'd have none of it.

Eventually, it became so much of a task that I bought her a car of her own just to give me a break from driving.

It was fun touring round the local garages. She said she fancied the little one-litre Vauxhall Nova and we looked around for something costing about £1500.

In the end, we passed a garage one day and she spotted a Vitara Jeep and the car that was going to cost me one and a half grand suddenly set me back a good deal more. But she loved it. It was brand, spanking new....white.....and it had 'Bernie' written on the front and back.

But this was more than a car to Bernie. The fact that I had splashed out my own money on something special for her in some way broke down that final barrier that existed between us.

I had made a commitment to her in pounds, shillings and pence. For her, the last bridge that had to be built between us just fell into place.

She gave herself to me.

Chapter Seven
Gaffer Trouble

IN my professional dealings with people, I would like to think of myself as a very reasonable individual; slow to anger and always ready to seek compromise, rather than confrontation.

While I have something of a reputation as a hard man on the pitch, it is simply not in my personal nature to pick fights.

However, there have been occasions at Celtic when my gaffers have encountered the rock-like principles on which I base my life. As a result of the fiercest, most heated altercations I can remember, I still can't believe my Celtic career didn't founder on those very rocks.

I have known three managers in my short time at Celtic Park. But the big barney I caused with Liam Brady was more about me than with me.

I think it was the comedian Jimmy Tarbuck who liked to poke fun at Gary Gillespie's run of injuries when he played at Liverpool. Tarby would trot out the gag that while all the other players at Anfield were given company cars, Gary Gillespie got an ambulance.

The same could have applied to me in 1991 after the disastrous, injury-hit start to my Celtic career. I was in the door just nine days when I ruptured my Achilles tendon during our 3-1 defeat by Hearts on 16 November.

While I managed to return for three games over the New Year period, including my Old Firm debut, that injury at Tynecastle was to haunt me for three months.

After playing in those games, when I was happy with most of my performances, I moved to hook a ball down the line, again against Hearts, on 4 January, and the ligaments in my other ankle just snapped.

Liam Brady was very, very frustrated that I could not get out there and do it. When he signed me, Tony Mowbray was to be the main man at the back, the man charged with plugging the leaky Celtic defence. He had spent a million pounds on me but due to sheer bad luck, that costly investment was lying flat-out on the treatment table.

It must have been all the more annoying for Liam that I had hardly missed a game through injury in almost 10 years at Ayresome Park.

Pressure began to build on him as the team were really struggling and, as usual, the gap between us and Rangers was becoming a chasm. We were 10 points behind the Ibrox club and 11 behind Hearts, who were going great guns.

The newspapers were unanimous: Brady's buys were flops. Flops, flops, flops.

I'm sure I would have enjoyed a good relationship with Liam had everything being going right for me on the park. That's usually the case between gaffers and players they've spent a bit of money on. But my prolonged absence from the team led to something of a tense atmosphere between us.

That was nothing compared to the atmosphere which developed between Liam and the Press in general and broadcaster Gerry McNee in particular. The two were appearing on Archie MacPherson's TV show 'Sport in Question' on 3 February 1992, just days after McNee had imparted some 'exclusive' news about my personal fitness.

The injury to Tony Mowbray, McNee had written the weekend before, was far more serious than Celtic had been admitting. Not just that, but it was so serious that he'd be out of contention for the rest of the season.

Liam had gone on the show with the sole intention of shooting that report down in flames. I remember watching the programme at home on TV. I had not played for a month by that time. Liam came as close to exploding as I've ever seen him.

He demanded to know the source of the information. Did Celtic have a mole at Parkhead? In any case, what did Gerry McNee know about Tony Mowbray? Tony Mowbray would be playing the next day! I did play the next day, in a friendly against New Zealand's international side at Parkhead. But I know my selection was more to prove Liam's point than anything else. I'm sure he rushed me back too soon, simply to fulfil his promises to Gerry McNee on TV.

We lost 1-0. I just happened to be the piggy-in-the-middle of their little argument. It was an argument that went far higher than the fitness of Tony Mowbray; Liam had, by this time, built up a terrible phobia about the Press. He hated how newspapers and telly would 'have a go' at the club.

For some time before the programme went out, I had been under pressure anyway to get back on to the park. It was a niggling injury. You would think that you were just about ready to go again when you would feel yourself pull up, the pain was too great.

But after the altercation on the airwaves, the pressure on me intensified. Before the game started, my leg was so heavily strapped up it looked ridiculous. Gradually, as the game wore on, the pain in my ankle would wear off. And once you get into the atmosphere of a game, you start to forget about any little feelings of pain that remain.

The Daily Record of January 5 reported: 'The injury agony for Celtic defender Tony Mowbray is over.'

I didn't play another competitive game for almost a month. Liam should never have committed me to that match.

Only subsequently did I discover that Liam and Gerry McNee ended the evening by going out for dinner to Pavarotti's together after the filming was over.

I genuinely felt sad the day Liam got sacked. The night before, in October 1993, we had gone down 2-1 at St Johnstone and I had played an absolute stinker. In my defence, I think I played a stinker because Liam had insisted on having just three at the back and I invariably find that set-up very difficult indeed. You end up getting pulled all over the place by nippy little wingers and I have to admit that pace has never been the strongest part of my game.

So I did feel partly responsible when I heard on the news he had been given the boot. After all, Liam was the one who had shown so much faith in me by bringing me to Celtic Park and paying £1 million for my signature.

I only had to wait a couple of weeks into new manager Lou Macari's reign for my next 'disagreement'.

Macari now admits that he was prepared to push me out of the Parkhead door within a month of becoming Celtic manager and, incredibly, without ever seeing me play.

Lennie Lawrence, the Middlesbrough manager, wanted to exercise the club's right to have first refusal on my signature if Celtic ever decided to sell.

It was 9 November 1993 and I was about to step on to the team bus heading to Pittodrie for a league match with Aberdeen, when Lou pulled me to one side for a 'quick chat'.

We went into his office and, out of the blue, Lou revealed that Lawrence had been on the phone to inquire about my availability and was travelling to Aberdeen to watch me that night.

Then he dropped another bombshell. He said: 'But I'm not going to play you!'

Whether he was worried that I could have played a stinker against Aberdeen and Lawrence might change his mind, I don't know. It was to be his first deal since taking over at Celtic and maybe he didn't want anything to go wrong.

But I know that Lennie was furious that here was I sitting next to him in the directors' box at Aberdeen, rather than shoring up the Celtic defence on the park.

He had travelled nearly six hours from Middlesbrough to see

me play and had told the Celtic manager that he was coming for that specific reason. He was beside himself with rage when he spoke to me at half-time.

In any case, he said he wanted to know how I felt about a return to my old club. I told him I didn't think the Pittodrie boardroom was the best place to discuss a transfer and we agreed that I would go down to Middlesbrough for a couple of days to see if there was something to talk about.

It was an exciting prospect. Bernie and I were about to be engaged. Here was the chance of setting up home together, furnishing a new house in a town I called home. I could show Bernie around Middlesbrough the way she had introduced me to Glasgow.

It all seemed set to go through. The clubs, I think, had agreed that I should be transferred but were still haggling over a price. They were talking in the region of £700,000, a drop of £300,000 on my price for going the other way two years previously.

Lennie and I had thrashed out my personal terms in the Middlesbrough boardroom. There was a weekly wage, a signing-on fee and a contract for a specific number of years.

Lennie thought it a lot for a Middlesbrough player to be on but the club was pushing for promotion and he believed that my return to the team could be the final piece in the jigsaw. If his side did go up, the financial rewards for the club could be enormous.

Bernie and I had been to see this marvellous house near Middlesbrough which was sat right on the golf course. There was a driveway of about 100 yards up to the front door; the back garden was practically on the fairway; it looked like South Fork in Dallas.

Bernie was almost on the point of ordering the curtains when we learned something had gone wrong in the financial negotiations between Lou and Lennie. I was owed money by Celtic for the remainder of my contract. I hadn't asked for a transfer so the club were duty-bound to pay me the outstanding amount.

First of all, it was suggested that the money I was owed should come off the top of the transfer fee which was payable by Middlesbrough. When that fell through, it was suggested that I forget about the outstanding amount owed to me.

There was no way I would be leaving Celtic if it meant I would be worse off. I had a contract, so why should I sell myself short? I would be happy to stay at Parkhead if that's what it meant. It was a point of principle.

I remember sitting in my mam's home down south, talking to Lou Macari in the phone. He was urging me to do the deal, saying things like: 'You'll never get a deal like this again; it's a one-off; take it!'

But I felt he was forcing me out of the club against my will. He said he wouldn't play me if the deal fell through; I'd spend my days in the Celtic reserves.

I was furious. I told him: 'I don't give a f*** about your team selection. I'll come back to Glasgow Celtic and I'll show you that I'm the best f****** defender you've got!'

I got back off the phone and thought: 'Wow! Did I really say that?'

Then, I realised my mam had been sitting on the stairs, listening to everything that had gone on. I cringed.

But instead of ticking me off for swearing in her house, she said: 'That's my boy. You told him, son.'

It had been a point of principle. And, incidentally, I did get back into Lou's team.

Maybe in the back of my mind, I knew it might not be the right move, anyway.

I have aspirations of management and I know how difficult it is to move from the dressing room to the manager's chair while at the same club. So I thought that if ever I was returning to

Ayresome Park, it would be as the gaffer.

Come June 1994, I was bidding farewell to my second Celtic manager. Lou Macari, the boss who had threatened to end my links with the club, was unceremoniously sacked by new supremo Fergus McCann.

If it came as a bolt out of the blue to many Celtic fans, it was merely the end to intense speculation which had been sweeping Celtic Park almost since he moved in.

The whispering would tell you: 'The board's going to change and wee Lou will be out the door, don't you worry about that.'

In the eight months he was at Celtic, he hardly endeared himself to the players. He was always telling us we weren't fit, insisting we go through these piggy-back exercises and carrying medicine balls around the training pitch for some reason.

Then there was his entourage. At times, it appeared he had brought so many back-room boys up from Stoke that there were more bodies in the dug-out than there were on the pitch.

It became a standing joke among the players, as we tried to work out each person's role in the grand scheme of things.

'Who the hell is that?' someone might ask of yet another new face in a track suit. 'Well what the hell does he do?'

It was when Celtic returned to Anfield for Ian Rush's testimonial game that I had my biggest bust-up with the current manager, Tommy Burns.

Headlines in the newspapers of 7 December 1994 left us humiliated. It was a Pearl Harbour of a result. The Daily Record thundered '6-0. Celtic Get the Bum's Rush' and they had to use a picture of yours truly on the back page, on my back-side, watching Rushie score number six!

To compound the agony, Liverpool's Mark Walters told the Press that his side had won easing up.

Most of the papers reported that the Celtic dressing room door remained closed for 50 minutes after the game. What was happening inside surprised even me.

Everyone got it in the neck from Tommy Burns. Defenders, mid fielders, attackers, we all felt the wrath of the manager. I cracked up.

I have very strong views about the way football should be played. That's why I think I could be a success at football management some time in the future. I just let Tommy know what I thought about his tactics; I let him have my opinions on his approach to the game and, shall we say, he let me have his views about my capabilities as a defender. It was the kind of heated discussion that often happens in football (when you've just been gubbed by six goals to nil).

I'm afraid that when the balloon does go up, I have to say what I feel until I've got it all out. Then, once Tommy and I had finished with each other, different players came in and started arguing among themselves.

To be honest, I think Tommy took a lot out of that exchange in the Anfield dressing room. Tactics changed from then on. He also voluntarily banned himself from the dug-out and chose to watch subsequent games from the stand.

But, again, it was a classic situation where I could have talked myself out of a job.

If he had misunderstood my motives and perceived what I'd said as a personal attack on him, then I'm sure I would have been out the door. I don't know if managers do respect you more as an individual if you are prepared to make a stand for something you believe in.

Just like the dispute with Lou Macari, Anfield was a point of principle.

And I wasn't going to surrender my principles. Not for anyone.

Chapter Eight
Crying in the Kit Room: The Horror of Finding Out

'BENGAL Lancer' – Peter Grant told me as if I should immediately understand what he meant. 'I'm sure it was Bernadette or her sister who had Bengal Lancer a couple of years ago.'

Call me naive. But a Scotsman using Cockney rhyming slang doesn't paint the clearest picture for a big bloke from the north of England.

We were in the car, on our way to training one morning, when my Celtic team-mate chose to inform me that the girl I was dating had once suffered from breast cancer.

There was no shock or horror on my part. It simply did not register. Cancer? My girlfriend? She certainly hasn't mentioned it.

It was only months later, when we became intimate, that I realised that she was fiercely defensive of her left breast. She never quite sat down and talked it through with me but I was to discover that she had suffered from breast cancer at the age of 22.

It also transpired that she was only just over the worst of her treatment the night I met her at Victoria's. She had been through the mill and was out on the town with her sister, determined to enjoy herself for the first time in months.

Experts have subsequently advised me that the incidence of breast cancer in a girl of 22 is one in ten thousand.

She had gone to Glasgow's Victoria Infirmary, complaining about a lump on her breast. Women are always being told to examine their breasts for lumps so she was doing the right thing. She was told to go away. Women of your age, they said, don't get breast cancer. They concluded that it was almost certainly a cyst, so they didn't do a biopsy. Nine months later, this thing on her breast was the size of an orange.

She had become embarrassed because, as I've said, she was the type of girl who would hug her friends a lot. And they'd pull back and say: 'What's that on your chest?'

She told the hospital she wanted this thing removed. They went in to take this so-called 'cyst' away and found a massive tumour.

Because they were not expecting to find cancer, they had to close her up again without touching it. When they did remove it, the stitches failed to hold and the wound opened up.

So, by the time I met her, a significant part of her left breast had been removed and she was left with this great scar down it, the result of being stitched up three times.

But since I was not around at the time, it's best to let her sister Elizabeth explain exactly what happened:

'It was when she was working at Pier 39, the bar on the banks of the Clyde in Glasgow's city centre, that Bernadette first told me that she had found a lump.

'At the time, I was a radiographer working at the city's Victoria Infirmary so I knew exactly what she should do. I told her to seek an appointment right away at the Victoria. .

'The appointment came through and I went to the hospital with her, but sat outside. When she did come out, she said to me: 'They said it's fine, just girl's trouble. There is nothing for me to worry about. I've just to come back in two months.'

'Two months down the line, the lump is getting bigger and again she went back, and again I went with her. She came out and she said they had told her the same thing as before.

'Shortly afterwards, she started being sick for no apparent reason, really violently sick. She could even be in her sleep but Bernadette would suddenly be violently ill.

'The fashion at the time was to wear tops with low necks and long sleeves but any time she wore something like that, people would ask her: 'Oh, what's that?' and they'd point to her lump.

When she went up to the Victoria for the third time and again, she said, she was told there was nothing to worry about, she insisted to the consultant that the lump should be removed.

'They gave her an appointment to come back, but it was an Out Patient's appointment. The doctor said hello to me when I walked on to the ward to pick up Bernadette and he looked puzzled when I began to leave with her.

'He asked me if I knew his patient and I replied: 'Yes, this is my sister.'

'He expressed his surprise and then moved as if he was going to say something to Bernadette; but something stopped him.

'Two days later, the consultant came to where I worked and told me: 'I really need to get your sister back in again. I've just had the results back from the operation to remove the lump.'

'I knew right there and then what he meant. You don't want to believe it, which is why I probably said something silly like: 'O.K. then.'

'It took a lot of persuasion to get Bernie to come back to the hospital. She said she couldn't leave her work, but eventually I convinced her that she had to get to the Victoria.

'Bernie's consultant came to see me after he had seen her. He told me: 'I have told your sister it is cancer.'

'Apparently, doctors told her that they had gone into her breast but were unable to remove the tumour because it was so big. They had to close her up again.

'She was so chirpy, it was unbelievable. She said doctors on the ward round had been telling her that she had cancer and she was saying to them 'Fine, now can I go back to work, please?'

'She said it was as if the doctors would only relax if she cried a bit. So she said she gave them a wee bubble and they seemed quite happy with that. After that, she had to have three operations under general anaesthetic before she got a 'clearance'. That's when they do a cytology test to make sure there are no cancer cells left in the area of the breast.

'Bernadette's problem was caused by the fact that her tumour was way back into the muscle of the breast, which meant that they had to scrape away some of the rib cage before they could get a 'clearance'. They just didn't appreciate at first how extensive the cancer was.

'Her breast had been massacred by these operations. Because she was so young, the hospital were suggesting silicon implants to restore her breast; maybe even plastic surgery.

'But once Bernadette got over the trauma of all that treatment, the physical appearance of her breast did not really trouble her.

'But she had tremendous spirit. At one stage, they thought they might have to remove the full breast and here's Bernie joking: 'I'll be on holiday on the beach and I'll have to shout 'Just one breast here, folks!'

'Some people were appalled by her sense of humour but I think it was the only way she could deal with what had happened to her, by being so flippant.

'I take the view that the the hospital should have carried out a biopsy of the lump straightaway to ensure that it was benign. But they didn't. Perhaps they should have given her a mammogram. But they didn't.

'They were saying that there are no known cases of someone of Bernadette's age developing cancer from a breast lump like she had.

'It was only after Bernadette's experience that the hospital's practice was changed to give biopsies and mammograms to EVERYONE with symptoms like hers.

'The hormones of young women are highly fertile, which means when cancer is present, it can race right through the body if it is not caught quickly. Bernadette was just 22.'

Bernie's brother, Danny, bought her a wee dog to cheer her up and she called it Chancer, to sound like the cancer she had left behind.

When Peter Grant broke it to me in his own, casual way, there was no sudden desire on my part to back off. There was no inner voice telling me: 'Beware, don't get involved.'

After all, the girl I was going out with was exciting, full of life. It was almost as if he was talking about someone else.

Anyway, our relationship developed and it was in the Autumn of 1993 that I decided I wanted to make her my wife. She had such an infectious personality. I wanted to be with her for the rest of my life.

Celtic had travelled to Portugal at the start of November for the second leg of the UEFA Cup clash with Sporting Lisbon.

After hearing the result on the radio, Bernie wrote me the following little note:

Dearest Darling 'Mog'

I have just had a nice, relaxing bath and dried my long black locks!!

It's 10 o'clock and my heart is pining for you. Shanks [Tony's dog] is next to me, laid by the fire. I am waiting for the sports at 10.20 p.m.; I feel sad for you and the team but another day, and another game.

I hope I sleep tonight. I might do, after hearing your voice when you phone tonight (I hope you are in good spirits because it will help me sleep).

Well, you will be home tomorrow and I can't wait to give you lots of kisses and cuddles and feel your lovely body next to me,

Looking forward to seeing you,
Love you always,
Bernie xx.

Having made the commitment in my own mind, all that

remained was to pick the right date to become engaged. The possibility that she might say no never even occurred to me. Her birthday was coming up the following April. Then there was always Christmas. I just thought: 'Bollocks, I can't wait that long. We'll get engaged on my birthday, 22 November'.

There's a ringmaker in Bothwell High Street. The girl there drew loads of designs and I agonised over which one to choose. I picked the diamond and I asked her to set a little emerald in the back of each ring. I thought that, 20 years down the line, this little emerald would remind us that when we became engaged, we were living in Glasgow and I was playing for Glasgow Celtic.

We flew down to London, on the pretext of celebrating my 30th birthday, and checked in to the Hilton Hotel on Park Lane. I took her to lunch at The Canteen, Michael Caine's restaurant at Chelsea Harbour.

I didn't get down on my knee or anything; I just waited until after the meal and produced the ring from my pocket. I just asked her, quietly: 'Will you marry me?' Thankfully, she didn't say no.

It was such a lovely moment. I'll always remember getting back to the hotel and phoning our parents to tell them. I could hear Irene, Bernadette's sister, whooping with delight in the background.

We were on top of the world, the perfect couple. I was lucky enough to have a well-paid job which meant we had sufficient money to indulge ourselves in any way we wanted. There would be plenty money for cars, holidays, a nice house. And to complete the ideal picture, we were so hopelessly in love with each other.

Within a few weeks, Bernie started complaining about a pain in her back. It had all the classic signs of sciatica but she was also beginning to lose a few days at work because of sickness.

She started going down with colds and mild flu, and then the pain started to spread to her leg and her hip.

It really embarrassed her, having to ask to leave her work because she was feeling unwell; she had hardly ever had to do that before.

At Parkhead one day, I had a chat with the club physiotherapist Brian Scott and described the symptoms to him. He thought it sounded like sciatica too, and even her GP in Barrhead reckoned that's what it was.

But the pain got worse and worse and I came in from training one day to find her bent double, the pain was so unbearable. I got her into the car and rushed her to Celtic Park. Without hesitating, Brian Scott referred us to Dr George Arbraimi, the club specialist who had treated my injuries in my early days with the club.

He looked at her and he knew within two minutes that it was not sciatica.

At his clinic the following day, Dr Arbraimi confirmed that Bernadette was not suffering from sciatica. It was very possible, he said, that it was cancerous.

Cancer? It can't be. Cancer was no longer part of our lives. This was something Bernie had left behind. It left me numb.

Dr Arbraimi said that he would have to explore that possibility because she had suffered from a form of cancer before. He wanted to do tests, X-rays and the like, so he would have to admit her to hospital. Bernadette had a real phobia about hospitals. Despite that, she agreed to be admitted to a ward at the Victoria with three other women, all considerably older than her. I went out and ordered her some flowers and headed off to training. Once I was finished, I called her on my mobile phone to say: 'Don't worry, darling, I'm on my way to see you.'

But she was crying on the phone and had to go into the toilet to speak to me because she was so upset. She said: 'I don't want to stay here . . . come and get me out.'

I had no choice but to drive to the hospital and sign my fiancee out against all medical advice.

She was still attending the Victoria for checks every three months, because of the breast operation she had undergone before. When she mentioned the back pain at her check-up in November, the doctor had decided to order a bone scan.

The results of those tests arrived almost at the same time as Dr Arbraimi's findings.

Little specks of cancer were showing up in the liver and lungs.

The implications didn't really hit us, to be honest. We just sat and hugged each other and I told her: 'You've managed to get over it before, darling; you'll do it again.'

But her sister, Elizabeth, looked a wee bit further into it. Her ears pricked up when the doctor said it was 'a secondary'.

A short time went by and as far as we were concerned, things had settled down. Bernadette had been given painkillers for her back trouble and they were working well. She had made arrangements to attend some radiotherapy sessions.

So I remember being really surprised one day when I turned up at Parkhead to find Elizabeth's husband, Gary Aitken, waiting for me in the car park. I thought: 'What the hell are you doing here?'

He said to me: 'Elizabeth wanted me to come and see you. You see, it's the cancer in Bernie's liver. It's going to be terminal.'

I walked into Parkhead, not knowing where I was. My head was in a whirl. I went into the players' changing room but I couldn't bear to sit there.

I had to go into the kit room, out of the way. Scottie, the physio, saw me go in and came after me. I burst into tears right there and then. A big guy like me. I was crying my eyes out. I was confused, bewildered by what I had just been told.

Suddenly, I didn't know what life was about any more.

Back at the house, Elizabeth sat with us on the floor of our living room and explained how this thing in Bernie's liver was going to kill her. The three of us sat and cried for about 15 minutes, just sat there on the floor. I'll never forget it. But then I just turned to Bernie and said: 'Look, love, we're going to get married.'

And she looked at me and said: 'Oh, Mog, can we?'

Chapter Nine
The Wedding:
Nothing but the Best for Bernie

ALL things being equal, Bernie would never have wanted a big wedding, complete with all the frills. Flowing wedding dresses, bridesmaids and a cake . . . she hated all that.

It had been her dream to fly to an island in the Caribbean, pull on some flimsy cotton dress and get married to me on the beach beneath a palm tree.

In fact, that's what we had been planning until news of her serious medical condition halted us in our tracks.

Our venue was meant to be Antigua in June, once the football season had finished. We had been so impressed by our time on the *Majesty of the Seas* the previous summer that we decided to book both sets of parents on a Caribbean cruise.

I am particularly close to my mam and dad, so Bernie and I thought it was important our parents should be there when we married.

We worked so hard to get it all booked. It exhausted the staff in the travel agents because we had to make sure that the ship docked for long enough in Antigua for them to attend the wedding. It then transpired that we had to be on the island at least nine days to qualify for a marriage licence.

We had only booked it about a week before we got the news about Bernie's cancer. After that, there was no way we could go ahead with our Caribbean Dream because doctors advised us to bring the whole thing forward.

I then embarked on a crusade to get everything ready for our big day. I told Bernie: 'Come on darling, we'll invite every single person you know to the wedding. It's going to be a day for everyone to see you in your prime.'

It meant that our wedding guest list went from four to more than two hundred.

The club, of course, had been marvellous about it all. Lou Macari was the Celtic manager at the time and he explained to me how he had been through the same thing with his dad, Albert.

Lou also gave me advice on how to handle the news with the media and we featured on the front and centre pages of *The Sunday Mail* on 20 March.

Bernie had asked *The Mail* to make the article as 'positive' as possible and she was delighted with the way it turned out.

She told *Mail* readers: 'It was a shock for everyone when I first got cancer because I was so young.

'You don't expect breast cancer to show up in someone until they are at least 35.

'It was a bigger shock that it's come back again so quickly. They thought I had got rid of it.'

But looking forward to her wedding she stressed: 'Despite the circumstances, I don't want it to be all doom and gloom.

'We've got a lot of friends so we want them all to make it a special day. I want people to be as positive as possible.'

We bought *The Mail* late on the Saturday night as we headed home from a night out in Glasgow. From the noises coming from her as she read it, I knew she was pleased.

Celtic basically left it up to me; if I wanted to play, they would be happy with that; if I felt unable to walk out in front of thousands of supporters, they would perfectly understand.

As it was, I chose to play and I even managed to score the final goal in our 3-1 victory over Dundee United the day before my wedding. The reason for me turning out in the Hoops was almost entirely down to Bernie; she asked me to continue with my game and do her proud.

The last words she would say to me as I would leave the

house were: 'Score a goal for me, darling. Kick the ball for Bernie.'

And that's what would keep me going during a game. You literally do go on the pitch and as the referee's about to blow the whistle to start the match, you do urge yourself: 'Come on, do it for Bern.' Sometimes you lose concentration during play and that is what I would always use as an incentive to snap back into the action: do it for Bern.

It's a terrible thing to admit, but I was not going out there and doing it for the other boys or this great institution called Celtic. I was doing it for my wife.

The one thing I did not do for my wife's sake was marry her. There was no sense of 'duty' on my part to wed this girl just because she had cancer and did not have long to live.

To do so would mean that you were not only deceiving yourself but Bernie as well. There is no way I would condemn myself to a lifetime of mourning for my wife just because it was a 'nice' thing to do.

You hear about these people who perhaps have second thoughts in the weeks leading up to marriage – the agony of wondering if they were doing the right thing.

There was nothing like that for Bernie or me. We both knew, one hundred per cent, that we wanted to become man and wife.

To let you know how much I loved her, I physically ached for the entire time she was away in Ireland after our fall-out. It actually hurt. There would be an emptiness, a great hole in my life whenever we were apart.

It's hard to believe, but I would even miss her when I was at training with the rest of the lads.

Whether that is what happens in the early stages of all young love, I don't know. But we felt we had something special.

For that reason, and the fact that she was not well, I decided I didn't want the groom's traditional stag night. I just didn't wish to be out of her company for five hours, leaving her at home with someone else. Although she hadn't yet started her chemotherapy, she was nonetheless suffering from the effects of the cancer itself, which meant that she could be sick at any time.

In fact, she was even sick on the aeroplane going down to London to choose her wedding dress. If the girl I love was going to find herself in embarrassing situations through no fault of her own, I wanted to be with her when they happened.

We travelled down with Jackie McQuade, Bernadette's head bridesmaid and best friend. It was a real laugh because I spent most of the day sitting outside changing rooms, listening to the giggles of two daft girls.

It was me who wanted to see her in a traditional wedding dress, something grand that would show off her lovely figure. She was so disinterested, it was me who would buy all the bridal magazines, 'Brides of Britain' and 'Bride and Groom' and the like, and casually leave them scattered about the house.

Even if she tried on something that was miles too big for her or had huge puffy-out shoulders, she and Jackie would come out of the changing room to give me a laugh.

Eventually, after going through everything that Harrods, Harvey Nichols and Armani had to offer, we went to Wizard of Gos, a specialist wedding shop in Kensington Square I had seen advertised in one of the magazines.

When Bernie, to my delight, picked something there, I had a quiet word with the boss, Elaine Gosling. Yes, I understood that these dresses normally take four to six months to create and; yes, I understand that you have dozens of other clients who booked before us.

I didn't like doing it, but I finally had to explain to Elaine that the reason we needed it so soon was because Bernie had cancer. Wizard of Gos dropped all of their other dresses to create one for my beautiful bride-to-be. They worked all the hours God sends to get it ready. We had it in a fortnight.

Technically, it was a pale ivory number, embroidered with

ribbon on lace. It had been voted London's 'dress of the year' by readers of Wedding Dress magazine. And it showed off her figure marvellously.

At first, we thought it would not be so easy to get hotels, cars and dress suits because these things get booked up six months in advance. But because we were getting married on a Sunday, Easter Sunday, 3 April, all those little difficulties disappeared.

The fact that it was not a Saturday also meant I was able to have my Celtic team-mates there as well. That was important to me as football is such a big part of my life.

I was absorbed by the arrangements. On top of the things most other couples have to organise, we had to apply for special permission for Bernie not to pass through the metal detectors at the airports we would use for our honeymoon in Cyprus.

Had we not done so, she would have been dreadfully embarrassed when the alarm was triggered by the electric pump on her Hickman Line. This is a drip that you carry around in a satchel which constantly feeds the chemotherapy treatment into your body.

Only Manchester City let us down on our big day. Even though they didn't have a game that day, City decided they could not release their player, Peter Beagrie, to be my best man at the wedding. Peter and I had been mates since we both played at Middlesbrough.

Man. City were near the relegation zone and they had a crucial league match at Southampton the following day, the Bank Holiday Monday. The club's management refused Peter permission to come to Glasgow on the Saturday and travel back to Gatwick and on to Southampton on the Monday morning.

It disappointed me because we felt there would have been time for him to make it down for kick-off but I suppose a club has to think about air delays and the like. Anyway, I took it better than Bernie did. She couldn't understand how people could be so cold and she felt bad for me because my choice of best man was not allowed to be there. In the event, my friend Martin Rodgers stood in at the last moment and did a fine job.

The bridesmaids were stunning: Jackie, Bernie's sister Irene, Jennifer Millar and Joyce Thomson. I still don't know how Bernie made it through the day.

When we first went to the Church to ask Father Benedict O'Keeffe to marry us, Bernadette had broken down in tears in front of him.

Only the month before, the priest had married Liz, Bernadette's sister, and Gary.

Rather than get married at St John's Church in Barrhead, Bernadette's local church with which she had lost contact, she thought it would be nicer to ask Father O'Keeffe for permission to marry at St Charles's R.C. Church in Paisley .

We went along with Liz to see him in his little office at the back of the church. Bernadette had been fine as we discussed the little details that you have to attend to, but suddenly she burst out crying for no apparent reason.

Father O'Keeffe is the most gentle, softly-spoken man you could ever wish to meet. He put his arm around her in the most loving way, trying to assure her that there was no need to be embarrassed about crying in front of him.

It was a very special moment. He was trying to put her at her ease and she was mortified that she had lost control of her emotions in front of a priest, of all people. That moment saw a bond forged between the two of them, a bond which was to become very special to her.

Because Bernadette was quite a difficult person to get to know, there were only three or four people she allowed into her life after terminal cancer was diagnosed. And Father O'Keeffe was one of them. I am sure marriage is an emotional time for any girl. But on the big day, you have also to remember that the decision to postpone chemotherapy until after the honeymoon meant that the cancer was spreading unchecked through her body. She had insisted to me: 'I don't want to be baldy on my wedding day.'

As a consequence, she limped, rather than walked down the aisle.

Father O'Keeffe revealed during the ceremony that the two of us planned to go to Lourdes to find a miracle cure for Bernie.

'So many people are praying for you,' he told Bernie.

'It seems as if the whole world has taken you to their hearts.'

There were smiles in the church when the priest turned to me and said: 'You scored a great goal yesterday, but it's nothing to the goal you scored today.'

Then it was back to the Moat House Hotel in Glasgow for the wedding reception. I'm sure loads of couples have ducked out of their reception in the past, but rarely have they done so for such poignant reasons as us.

Bernie had been absolutely drained by the experience. I knew how weak she had been on ordinary days, as the cancer wore her down. But all eyes had been on her all day, there was the need for the wedding pictures at Glasgow's People's Palace and then she sat through the meal and all the speeches. I knew she could even have been ill coming up the aisle. She was shattered.

Bernie would have loved to have stayed at the reception longer.

She was surrounded by her friends and her family, people who had known her all her life and had come to see her wed.

But, once the speeches were over, the two of us had to head off to bed. And within a minute of her head hitting the pillow, she was asleep.

The party went on until well after midnight. I've seen the video and it seemed everyone was having a great time. The gaffer, Tommy Burns, was there. He and his wife don't have to be told twice that the jigging has started, so there he was on the tape, dancing away.

It did not trouble me that I was upstairs in bed. I had married my Bernie.

I was the proudest man in the world.

Chapter Ten
The Question No-one Should be Asked

THE awful truth about Bernie's predicament was known to us, right from the day when we sat down with Elizabeth and cried our eyes out. We knew, but we didn't talk about it.

There was this unwritten rule between us and the people around us.

We would try to be positive in everything we did and said. When she got low, I would squeeze her hand, look her in the eye and tell her: 'Don't worry, darling, our miracle will happen.'

That would make her smile.

We even received cards and letters from people who had learned about Bernie's illness, recommending some form of miracle cure. Some would even finish their letter with something like: 'Now that I have told you what the cure is, I won't write to you again until I read in the papers that it has worked.'

Bernadette received a lovely letter from Rosemary Burns, the wife of Tommy Burns who was still manager of Kilmarnock at the time.

She told Bernie about a special statue of Our Lady in which a great many people had enormous belief. It was called the Rosa Mystica, and Catholics claimed that praying to her had resulted in special favours being granted to the sick.

The Burns family had heard about the statue's remarkable properties and sent off to Italy for one of their own. They prayed to the Rosa Mystica for Rosemary's young cousin, whose baby was born with cerebral palsy and who was not expected to enjoy a great quality of life.

The family, among others, all said their Novena to the Rosa

Mystica for nine consecutive nights, beseeching her to allow the child to grow up healthy.

Tommy told us that the child is now four years old and is one of the smartest wee kids you could find.

Another member of Tommy's family developed cancer. Again they prayed for her and she was cured. Not surprisingly, Tommy and Rosemary have enormous faith, not necessarily in the statue, but in the power of prayer before it.

In the letter to Bernadette, they offered to lend us the statue for as long as we needed it. And, of course, we accepted.

Bernadette's story travelled the world after our problem was first highlighted in *The Sunday Mail*. The Catholic newspaper, *The Universe*, picked it up and as a result we started getting letters from places like Zimbabwe and Nigeria.

People we never even knew were telling us that they had left flowers in some church somewhere in Africa, with a prayer for Bernadette attached. There were thousands of letters.

Correspondence came in from all over America. One of the more promising ones told me about an Australian doctor, a Mrs Snook, who had written a book on how diet changes can bring about remarkable results.

I waited until about 11 o'clock one night to phone Australia, so that Mrs Snook would be at her work. I sent off for her book and an assortment of dietary sheets.

According to them, Bernadette should not touch meat, but eat raw vegetables straight from the earth. There should be coffee enemas to flush out her intestine. This process would cleanse the body, de-toxify it. The principle which underlined all these treatments was that if the cancer can't feed on toxins, it can't keep growing.

I immersed myself in all sorts of books, promising all sorts of cures. Orders were sent off to book shops all over the world. I had Bernadette believing that it was just a matter of finding the right remedy.

Because, once you give in mentally, you can chuck it in altogether. We never got to that stage. The only time there was a recognition that we might be parted came when we had to choose inscriptions for our wedding rings.

Without coming right out and saying it, our messages of love on those bands of gold told the full, sad story. They read 'Eternal Love, Mog' and 'Eternal Love, Bernie'.

Near the end, she would again try to cheer me up. She had amazing strength of character. She would tell me: 'No matter what happens, Tony, I will always be your guardian angel. I'll always be there on your shoulder, watching over you.'

I simply wouldn't let her talk about death. The miracle was going to happen. Yes, she had cancer but she would get over it the way she had got over it before.

As cold as it may seem, we actually sat down before any treatment began and discussed with doctors whether she should undergo any chemotherapy treatment at all; we knew what she was going to be like; we knew how her body would react.

The questions themselves were simple. Is the quality of life going to be any better with chemo? Or does going without treatment mean a shorter life span but a better quality of life for the time that she's alive?

If you were to stop and think about it, these are questions no couple should be asked to answer. You are effectively being asked to decide between life and death.

We seriously considered rejecting any chemotherapy at all to avoid the horrible side-effects we knew she would suffer.

But Dr Donald Bissett, Bernie's oncologist from the Beatson Institute, was adamant. Violently unpleasant as it was, chemotherapy slowed down the advance of cancer. Put simply, it bought us time.

Of course, when we got home and sat down and thought about it, there never really was an option. Every extra day we could spend together, holding hands, was a blessing.

Dr Bissett has the extraordinary talent of putting people at their ease, despite the tragic reasons for finding yourselves in his company. You somehow felt safe when he was talking to you.

I even remember things going wrong at our home and thinking: 'Oh, everything would be OK if Dr Bissett was here.'

I honestly don't want to scare anyone reading this who is either suffering from the early stages of cancer or who has a loved one who is.

The vast majority of the medical staff who treated Bernie were thoughtful, considerate individuals. Some of them became our friends. Bernadette even sent me out at Christmas to buy a present for Dr Bissett.

But I do feel bad that Bernadette did not have an easy time of it, from a treatment point of view. She suffered a hell of a lot. It seemed to be just one thing after another. Things went wrong from day one. She was in hospital to have the Hickman Line attached to her. You go back to the hospital once a week to have it changed.

It was just one of the two ways chemotherapy would be given to her; the other method was by injection.

When they put the Hickman Line in, they punctured her lung.

The line was inserted while I was there, and the screams of pain from Bernie were unbelievable. She was supposed to stay in the Western Infirmary overnight and I left her in the ward, after visiting time, around 8 p.m.

They hadn't realised her lung had been punctured at the time and I got a phone call from the hospital at home at about 11.30 p.m. The nurse told me Bernadette was shouting out for me; 'she needs you'.

I went straight off into the night and settled down to sleep in what would become a familiar armchair to me, right beside her bed.

Her lung collapsed three times that night. The doctors told me that you deal with a punctured lung by piercing a hole in the patient's side, inserting a tube through the rib cage into the lung and allowing the air to drain out. But it transpired that the diameter of the first tube they used on Bernadette was not big enough.

She was in agony. She dug her nails into my hand as they inserted this tube into her side. The pain must have been horrendous because she made my hand bleed, her nails dug in so deep.

So it was even worse, a few hours later, when her lung collapsed again. They had to pull the damn thing out again and put another, bigger, one in.

The tube is fed into a bottle on the floor. When it stops bubbling, it means the lung has fully re-flated. Six days later, this bottle was still bubbling.

They got a lung specialist to look at Bernie. He said the tube STILL wasn't big enough so it had to come out again. This specialist was very, very good but removing the tube for a third time still caused Bernie a lot of pain. You have to ask why they didn't get an expert to put the tube in in the first place.

Bad luck became so much the norm for us that we used to laugh and I'd say: 'Oh well, darling, what's one more problem after what we've been through?'

But I had got a real fright that night, being called to her bedside and seeing her in so much pain. It was now becoming apparent why Bernie had such a phobia about hospitals.

Because of her fears, we made sure she was never left alone in hospital from that time. If I had to head off for training of a morning, Elizabeth would come and sit with her.

Despite my worldwide search for a cure, Bernadette never really got the chance to try any of those radical diets.

She was desperate to live; desperate to live for us. So she would be willing to try anything if it gave her the chance of a medical breakthrough.

I would go to these health food shops and buy up things like organic tomato juice and pulses. But after the hard times she had in hospital, she was physically in no fit state to go on any diet. In fact, they put her on steroids to build her up again.

That was the time when football really went out of the window for me. I could never have played again and I would not have cared.

But again, Bernie was the one urging me to trot off to Parkhead. She'd say: 'Away you go and get me some gossip about the other players. Off you go.'

Chemotherapy is a horrible thing. I can't emphasise enough the terrible transformation it wreaks on the person receiving it.

I know it buys time. It gives you longer with the one you love.

And Bernie's energy levels shot up after her treatment began, as the mixture began to attack the cancerous cells.

But to see someone you love suffering within minutes of the fluid entering the body is painful in the extreme.

Bernadette had undergone chemotherapy when she was found to have breast cancer at the age of 22. It was given to her at intervals of three weeks. Apparently she would be sick for the first week after treatment, be as good as new during the second week and then sick again in the third week in anticipation of the next round of treatment.

Whether it was psychological, I don't know. But from the first day of injection treatment after our wedding, Bernadette was violently ill.

As soon as the first of five different substances was injected into her arm by the IV nurse, Bernie could detect this terrible, metallic taste in her mouth.

She was sick there and then. Back home, I put her to bed and we had about an hour's respite from the sickness before it started again.

It then went on for a total of 22 hours, with Bernie being

105

violently ill every half hour. Right through the night. Right through the day.

Of course, it would get much worse the longer it went on because she had nothing left in her stomach.

Her vomiting would go on for up to 15 minutes, in total agony because there was nothing left to bring up. It would come up as black bile or blood.

And the distress of watching your wife suffering such extreme discomfort simply defies description. It was horrific as the clock ticked by and you thought: 'Oh no, here it comes again'.

The following day, things had 'improved' because she might only be sick six or seven times in the day. The vomiting would steadily decrease so that, by the end of the week, she stopped being sick at all.

Bernadette underwent two sessions of chemotherapy by injection but it was no use; her body's reaction was too severe. Again, we went through the debate about whether we should or whether we shouldn't.

But then, unfortunately very late in her illness, we discovered an alternative way that chemotherapy can be applied to the body. They take you in to hospital, drug you to the point of near-unconsciousness and slowly feed the chemotherapy by drip into the body. The Hickman Line is additional to this.

For Bernie, it worked a treat and she had her last four chemotherapy sessions that way.Living in the hospital became a way of life for us. It was in stark contrast to the life we had been leading just a year before, when we had our fabulous holiday in Florida and the Caribbean. Then, fit and healthy, we could have taken on the world together.

But drowsy as she was, I knew it was a comfort to her that she could feel my hand on hers, coaxing her on. In those circumstances, it doesn't matter that she's unwell; you are together for another day.

I seriously thought we were going to go on like that forever. I know the frustration of people who might have a Down's Syndrome baby or a mentally-handicapped person in their family.

But they are so lucky. Just to have them there.

I would have given anything to have kept hold of Bernadette, even if she had been in that state, for the rest of my life.

Drugged, drowsy, sick or whatever, I would have accepted that.

Anything that would keep her by my side.

Chapter Eleven
Raith Rovers – the Lows and Highs of Ibrox

I'VE had many disappointments in my footballing career. As a youngster, I broke a leg in a trial for England Schoolboys. There was the time I missed out on that Cup Final at Wembley. And there was also the trauma of my long lay-off through injury at Celtic. Then there was Raith Rovers.

At Ibrox on 27 November 1994, the stage was set for a glorious reversal of Celtic's fortunes. The team had qualified for the Coca Cola Cup Final by beating Aberdeen in a marathon semi-final, again played at the home of Rangers.

Raith Rovers were the pride of Kirkcaldy but they were coming from the First Division and had only made the Final by beating Airdrie (on penalties). Surely this was the platform from which The Bhoys would re-launch their mission to become a dominant force in Scottish football again.

On a personal basis, I was desperate to win the first winners medal of my career. But more than that, I wanted the Cup for Bernie.

For it was only through the will of Bernadette that I had maintained my links with football during the difficult months of 1994. When your wife is dying of cancer, somehow football doesn't seem to matter.

Frankly, I was ready to chuck it in completely. What need did I have for training? What was the point of running around a pitch for 90 minutes after a daft ball? I had a wife who needed me; who loved spending time with me. And time was running out.

It was Bernadette who insisted that I keep myself fit. She would hound me out the door of a morning, telling me that her sisters Mary or Elizabeth would be round to sit with her.

And, to be honest, it was a release for me. I would have a couple of hours on the training ground, where I would try to clear my head in the fresh air. Any of the boys in the team will tell you I was completely hopeless, unable to concentrate.

I didn't look like a footballer at all. The gaffer, Tommy Burns, knows I had some disastrous days at training. There was a five-a-side game one day when I might not have been on the pitch for all the contribution I made.

Then it was into the shower, change and back to Bothwell to spend the other 22 hours of the day with my wife. Most of the time I was speeding out of the car park before the other lads were changed.

Having said that, I think I was in a good frame of mind for the Coca Cola Cup Final. Tommy Burns had given me added incentive to play well.

If Celtic won the Final, he promised, I would be allowed to take The Coca Cola Cup home in victory to my Bernie. He'd even let us keep it overnight in the house.If that was the fairy-tale script that fateful Sunday, then nobody showed it to the boys from Fife.

Charlie Nicholas had put us 2-1 up with just six minutes left to play. There should have been no way back for Raith then.

But for some reason, we started to fall deeper and deeper back into our own half, almost inviting them to come at us. I've seen it plenty of times during my career. A team goes a goal up and instead of being buoyed by the advantage, it seems to introduce the dreaded 'fear' factor into their play.

This explanation could apply to Celtic that day. There was enormous pressure on us to win; not only would it mean the first trophy for the club in five years – it was an automatic passport to European football the next season.

We were suddenly fearful of losing all that and as a consequence we retreated too far into our own territory.

I could see it coming. As the seconds ticked away, I was bawling to get our players forward because our mid field was sitting right on top of our defence, almost asking them to attack us.

Because play was taking place so far into our half of the field, when a free kick was conceded, it was only 25 yards from our goal.

Just before the equaliser went in, I remember thinking: 'Oh, no, this is too deep.'

Gordon Dalziel sent a diving header past Gordon Marshall in the 87th minute to put the game into extra time. And after a further 30 minutes, when the tie was still drawn, it was all down to penalties.

Raith Rovers had scored with six of their shots; we had scored with five but it was our turn to take. I remember watching Paul McStay walk up to take his penalty. I was thinking: 'This is his destiny. Either he'll score and we'll go on to win the Cup, held aloft by Captain Courageous Paul McStay or, as happened, he misses and his whole world caves in on him.'

Paul McStay will recover from that day. He has the strength of character and a supportive family behind him to ensure that he does.

I am aware there were terrible scenes all around the ground. After all, 35,000 Celtic supporters had come along for this lap of honour after five traumatic years. Apparently, fans were pulling the green-and-white hats off the heads of their sons and throwing them onto the park. I saw none of it because I lay for hours in the Ibrox bath afterwards, unwilling or unable to get out.

The frustration of the fans was understandable. We had fought our way to the Final of a major competition. We were playing Raith Rovers, of all teams. Anyone will tell you that we should have won that game. And won it comfortably.

Anyway, I got home and Bernie is waiting for me, all bubbly

and bouncy. She was trying to cheer me up, would you believe?

But I was so disappointed. I had come home without The Cup.

But if Ibrox was the scene of my greatest footballing 'low' in Scotland, it appears it was also the venue for my greatest triumph. At least, according to my old gaffer, Lou Macari.

This is his account of the day I soared in his estimation:

'Tony Mowbray could have been lost to Celtic in November 1993 and it would have been an absolute disaster for the club . . . and for me.

'I had arrived as manager at Parkhead just a month before and had not even had the opportunity to see him play. But the knives were out for him for some reason and there were several people at Celtic who were urging me to get shot of him.

'I am not sure, but it may have had something to do with the fact that he was English.

'As the new arrival, having been in England for my entire managerial career, I had to rely on advice from people who were in with the Parkhead bricks. The same people were telling me that John Collins and Paul McStay can't play in the same team.

'There was an enquiry from Tony's old club, Middlesbrough, who had first option on him if ever we decided to sell. Foolishly, I allowed them to talk to Tony and was quite prepared to let him go for around £700,000.

'In any case, the deal fell through and it was fully five months later that I realised what a mistake his departure would have been.

'It was the last week of April 1994 and the final Old Firm meeting of the season was fast approaching. Rangers had decided to ban Celtic supporters from their ground because of damage to seats at Ibrox some time in the past.

'Everyone connected with Celtic knew that Tony Mowbray's mind would be on other matters. News of Bernadette's illness had hit the papers the month before and the couple married in

111

Paisley on April 3. As is usual for the run-up to the Rangers game, we took the players down to Seamill to hopefully remove them from any distractions and allow us time to concentrate on the challenge ahead.

'Tony, of course, chose to stay at home with Bernadette. From the moment I found out about her illness, I told him to do whatever he thought was right. Sure, I needed his presence in the team but that paled into insignificance compared to the need his wife had of him.

'I couldn't believe it then when I received a message on the morning of the game from Tony Mowbray. He wanted to play at Ibrox and could the team bus please pick him up at the MacDonald Hotel on its way up from Ayrshire?

'The atmosphere on the bus was pretty weird anyway. Because of the ban, the Celtic directors chose to boycott their places in the Rangers directors' box. I think there were just 15 of us on the coach when we picked up Tony in Giffnock.

'In some ways, I could have understood his readiness to play if he had been with us for two or three days before the match. It would have given him time to focus on his game, to enjoy a bit of camaraderie with the other lads.

'But this guy was with his dying wife up until about 12.45 p.m. that Saturday, 30 April, and here he was at 1.30 p.m. on a bus heading to a match where he'd be facing 50,000 rival supporters.

'WELL IT JUST HASN'T HAPPENED BEFORE!

'I didn't know how he would react. There is bound to be a doubt in your mind about how this fella is going to cope. You are ready to accept that he is simply not able to perform in those circumstances and if I had got anything out of him that day, it would have been a bonus.

'As it was, he played like a giant. Deflected in no part by the hostile atmosphere of Ibrox with no green-and-white backing, Tony Mowbray led by example in holding our defence together.

'It was painfully clear to me that this was someone not just playing for the team; he was out there playing for his Bernadette. And it seemed to make him rise above the occasion.

'John Collins scored with a quite extraordinary free kick with his new Predator boots. We were within 10 minutes of taking the points when Alexei Mikhailichenko grabbed the equaliser.

'But Tony Mowbray was the man of the match.

'He had not only come through a football game, he had passed a supreme test of character.

'Perhaps I appreciated more than most the anguish he must have been going through. I told him that my dad, Albert, had been diagnosed as suffering from cancer within a few weeks of me signing for Celtic in 1967.

'Initially, I had been told that my dad had just six months to live, but in the end he survived for six years.

'We were grateful for every day. I would go home at night from Parkhead and give my dad a massage to help ease the pain. One night, near to the end, I found that the muscle and tissue I had been massaging the day before had disappeared.

'It was a very traumatic time for all our family so it meant I had some understanding of what Tony must have been suffering.

'But he is a strong man. He will play again and he will play well. Tony Mowbray will come back from this, perhaps stronger than ever.'

I came to Scotland completely oblivious to the depth of rivalry that exists between Celtic and Rangers. I knew them to be poles apart but then Manchester is split between United and City, and Liverpool people will either follow the reds or the blues of Everton. By nature, teams will command their own sections of support from the same city.

We've even seen Liverpool and Everton fans travelling in the same car if they've been playing in a final at Wembley.

So I had no reason to think Glasgow was any different. How wrong I was. Right from the day I joined the club, people would come up to me and encourage me to play well in the Old Firm game at New Year. It didn't seem to matter to them that this was only November.

As it happens, I even scored in my first match against Rangers, the clash at Parkhead on 1 January 1992. To fans I met in the days after the game, it didn't seem to matter too much that they had lost 3-1. They would pat me on the back and say: 'Great goal, big man. We could be doing with more like that.'

When we ran out onto the pitch at Celtic Park, I remember being stunned by the sheer colour of the spectacle. I know players fresh to this tie normally recall it for the noise it seems to generate, but for me it was the sight of all those Union Jacks and Tricolours that took my breath away.

The flags were everywhere, draped over every available piece of board or hoarding. A sea of green, white, gold, red and blue. And they were massive flags, much bigger than anything we had seen to date in England I actually think that the televising of this one fixture probably led to the huge upsurge in English fans taking flags to games.

It was a cracking match, set alight just before half-time by Ally McCoist tapping home a mis-hit shot by Mark Hateley. Four minutes after the re-start, I equalised with a snap header from a corner by Mike Galloway.

I could easily have been sent off for the enthusiasm of my celebrations; I had been booked earlier in the game but I couldn't resist leaping over one of the advertising boards behind the Rangers goal.

The referee took no action and the goal really put us back into the game. We should have won it but our keeper, Gordon Marshall got caught up with McCoist in a crazy scramble for the ball at the Rangers end and Ally went down in the box.

Hateley scored from the penalty in the 77th minute (the only goal he's ever scored when I've been playing) and they didn't really look back. John Brown gave them a third, just a minute from full-time. *The Daily Record* seemed impressed by my derby day debut. Their Monday morning summary gave me four stars out of five and judged: 'Tough guy in defence and his goal gave Celts a chance.' My initiation into this ancient rivalry left me in no doubt just how important it is to both sets of supporters. And that, to me, is what football is all about. The games that really matter to your supporters.

Sadly, by signing big names like Terry Butcher and Ray Wilkins in the mid-1980s, Rangers spectacularly beat Celtic to the punch. And it's a blow from which the Parkhead club has never really recovered.

In one neat operation, Graeme Souness injected into the dressing room a most potent drug . . ..the feeling of success.

These were men who had played for England, for goodness' sake – winners who know what it's like to win and know what it takes to win.

What we now need at Celtic Park is a complete change of attitude, a belief that the major honours in the game are there for the taking. I don't want to do the manager's job for him but if the money is available, I believe we should be going out there and buying winners, players of quality, the proven article.

Don't go out and buy potential because that potential will just get swallowed up in the maelstrom of not winning anything, the way that Stuart Slater got swallowed up.

Get someone who is big enough and strong enough to rise above everything and get the whip out to other people in the team. We need a leader. But I am crucially aware that the principle I am advocating was tried by Liam Brady in his first season at Parkhead. He bought Gary Gillespie, a player who had won a string of league and cup honours with Liverpool. But even Gillie is disappointed with the way things worked out.

He would have been the right player if Celtic had won the

title or the Scottish Cup the following year. So, yes, go out and spend £2million on Ian Wright of Arsenal . . . but make sure you then go on to win a major domestic honour.

If we had the money, I'd love to see Celtic go out and buy Alan Shearer from Blackburn and Paul Ince from Manchester United. I rate Paul Ince the best player in Britain. He's a winner all the way. You can see he's the inspiration behind Manchester United.

But then, I don't suppose we've got £20 million to spare, have we?

That's not to say Celtic don't have some fine young talent coming through, especially in the shape of little Brian McLaughlin and Simon Donnelly.

In my first two seasons at Celtic, I would be playing frequently in the reserves as I battled back from yet another injury. I have known for a while that I will be aiming for a job in football management once my playing career is over.

So, during the reserve games, I remember making a mental note of Brian and Simon: 'Right, if those two boys haven't made it by the time I've become a manager, I'll be on to the Celtic gaffer like a shot'.

Simon had a sensational start in Celtic's first-team, so much so that the Press were hailing him as 'the new Kenny Dalglish'.

Two goals against Manchester United at Old Trafford, which Simon scored in Mark Hughes' testimonial game in May1994, is bound to get you noticed.

He received a lot of adulation, followed by sacks of fan mail and perhaps he could be forgiven for thinking: 'Wow, I've made it.'

But everyone said his second season was going to be the big test for him and I'm afraid that, mainly because of injury, he's had quite a dreadful time of it since starring at Old Trafford. After such a brilliant start, he's come down to earth with an almighty bang and I'm sure he knows next year could be a crucial time for him. He's a level-headed boy and I am sure he's up to it. If Celtic are to mount a serious challenge to Rangers supremacy in the run-up to the next century, everyone connected with the club has to hope that Simon does battle through.

In terms of our rivalry with Rangers, Celtic fans might not like me saying so, but I don't think that that depth of rivalry extends to the majority of players on the two sides.

One of the nicest guys you will meet is Ian Durrant, the Rangers mid fielder. We went to a couple of weddings where we were in his company and he couldn't have been more friendly.

We were even invited to Ian and Angela's wedding up in Hamilton in June 1994 but Bernie was going through her chemotherapy at the time and didn't want the embarrassment of perhaps being sick in front of other guests. She chose not to go to Angela Walker's hen night in Glasgow for the same reason.

We've even been out shopping in Glasgow and bumped into Ally McCoist and his wife; so we've all trotted off to the Princes Square shopping mall together for a coffee and a chat.

No matter what goes on during the 90 minutes on the park, it all boils down to the fact that you are just two guys who are doing the same job. And that's why when you meet another recognised player, whether you know them or not, you usually find you get on well and have plenty to talk about.

After Bernie's illness became public, there was the odd piece of abuse thrown at me from Rangers supporters.

But when you consider you are talking about one or two people out of 42,000 who regularly turn up at Ibrox, you can see what a tiny minority the nut-case really is.

To show the other side of human nature, we even received wedding cards from people saying they had been Rangers supporters all their lives but wished the two of us all the happiness in the world.

I'll remember that.

Chapter Twelve
Movies at Midnight

THERE were a couple of months in the autumn of 1994 when I seemed to be financing the British video trade almost single-handed.

Bernie had gone onto a treatment of steroids, aimed at building up the body that had been decimated by a combination of cancer, chemotherapy and medical cock-up.

I am glad that the doctors had agreed to put her onto steroids; it gave her a bit more dignity in her final months as her weight started to pile on again. But the start of the treatment signalled a seemingly endless period of sleepless nights and dreadful exhaustion which that deprivation inevitably brings.

Bernie discovered two side-effects of her steroid treatment: she couldn't sleep and she was eating like a horse.

We would watch the 2 a.m. movie on Sky and as soon as that was finished, she'd say: 'Go downstairs, darling and make me spaghetti on toast.'

There was no way I could argue with her. 'OK, darling,' I'd say. 'No problem.'

We would then begin to watch the 4 a.m. movie and I'd be sent downstairs to get her a bacon sandwich. By the time the 6 a.m. movie began, I'd be stood there in our kitchen, eyes popping out of their sockets, fixing Bernie a plate of scrambled egg on toast.

I am sure she must have seen every single tape in the video shop in Bothwell High Street. She loved films based on true stories and the video shop has an entire section devoted to that kind of movie, about 200 in all. We saw every single one.

Some times, I'd come home at night with six tapes under my arm and I'd take them back the next day, having seen them all from start to finish. It would get to the stage where I could not keep my eyes open; I would try to watch the film with her because she loved being able to talk about a particular scene or the way a storyline was developing. I could hardly share her excitement. I was knackered.

But if my body was telling me to take the sleep it craved, my mind was a constantly ringing alarm clock. I needed to be with her and if that meant keeping my eyes open with matchsticks, then so be it.

I would be dead on my feet. I'd sit up all night, keeping Bernie company and go to training the next day looking like a complete zombie.

I couldn't blame her. We both knew that it was the steroids working on her. It wasn't her fault. But inevitably, when you are as tired as I was, frustrations would gnaw away at you and you would eventually blow up.

There were times when I would lose my temper with her. But I am not a violent man so it never came to anything more serious than a bit of a shouting match in our bedroom.

At times, I would yell at her: 'Leave me alone! I'm not going downstairs to make you beans on toast. It's four o'clock in the morning and I've been down three times already!'

I would go to sleep just to spite her but I would wake up half-an-hour later with Bernie tickling the soles of my feet or gently scratching my back.

But if I was able to hold back from any form of physical violence, the steroids made sure that Bernie could not. Her dosage steadily progressed from a half of a milligram to eight milligrams of steroids a day. I used to take some terrible beatings from her, purely the result of frustration and the strong drugs working on her body.

She would walk right up to me and batter me hard in the face. I would have to stand there and take it, getting smashed in the mouth or on the side of the head by my darling wife. I couldn't get angry with her when she did that. I knew it was the steroids. It was as if it was a totally different person.

The sad part was, maybe and hour or so later, she'd realise what she had done and she would be so full of remorse. She loved her husband, Mog. There was no way she wanted to hurt him but this was what drugs had done to her.

Soon, I was so wracked with tension and physical exhaustion that I simply wasn't functioning at the club. I was losing weight and found it difficult to concentrate on anything.

It didn't help when a tatty English tabloid splashed news of my gaunt appearance over the front page. The story read:'He looks a withered shadow of his normally-sturdy self. He has had to miss two matches because of his illness.'

WHAT DID THEY EXPECT?

If I remember correctly, Bernie didn't even see that story. You see, by this time I was shielding her from any of the articles which appeared in the Press which I considered unhelpful.

I fully realised that because of my position at Celtic, Bernadette's plight was likely to interest the newspapers.

To be honest, I think it's sad that journalists have to wait until the wife of a Celtic footballer falls ill before they will write about breast cancer.It's a huge killer and the vast majority of women bear it with enormous dignity. Why can't these journalists go visit a cancer ward and write about the bravery that is evident every day of the year?

What I call bravery is a woman like Bernadette, her arms and legs so bruised from needles, needles, needles that there simply wasn't anywhere left on her body to take blood from. And still she could smile.

Bernadette's story had been fully reported. It detailed what, medically, was expected to happen to her, so I could see no point in some newspapers describing her as 'dying footballer's wife, Bernadette Mowbray'.

Any piece that referred to 'death' in any way was bombed

out. She would ask why a particular newspaper was not lying around the house and she'd smile, realising that I had been editing it.

Maybe these people don't appreciate that the words they tap out in their air-conditioned offices can have a devastating effect on their subjects.

Feature writers wrote sensitive letters to us, asking if they could come and do an interview; some even wanted to come up from London. And Scottish Television did their level best to get us to appear on Kirsty Young's Show. But the answer was the same to them all . . . No!

After months of sleepless nights, we eventually had to ask Bernie's sister, Irene, to stay over at our house before games so that I could get some shut-eye.

On Friday nights, I would pack the two of them off into our bed and I'd crawl into the single bed in the spare room for what I hoped would be a night of blissful repose. More often than not, I would turn the light out, slip in between the sheets, only to discover the bed had been covered in a disgusting mixture of toothpaste, crisps and broken biscuits. I would let out an almighty scream as I rolled in this mixture.

Then I would hear the laughs and giggles of the two girls in the next room who had planned and executed the whole dastardly deed.

Bernie loved her little joke. Even though she was in constant pain – to let you know how bad it was, she was taking about 16 tablets a day – her happy, bubbly nature would shine through.

I had bought her a wig as some form of compensation for the loss of her own hair, due to the chemotherapy. It's a shame. It's only when you start to lose it quickly that you realise how much hair you have on your head. And Bernadette's was such lovely hair.

We were lucky to find a wig with exactly the same colour as Bernie's own hair. You could even brush the fringe the way she used to have it. It was perfect. I got a hairdresser out to the house to cut it in her style.

Unfortunately, Bernie wouldn't wear it because she thought it was daft. I had to do my bit to reduce the embarrassment she was feeling at losing her lovely, flowing tresses – the theory being that if she knew her man still thought she was gorgeous, then the loss of her hair was somehow easier to bear.

One day, I tried the wig on and to be truthful, I thought I looked quite good in it. It seemed to sit nicely, its colour starkly in contrast to the little beard I would try to grow quite long.

She would go into hysterics every time I pulled it on. And that's when she hit on the idea for me to take it into work one day wearing it on my head.

I walked into Parkhead that morning as if it was the most natural thing in the world. I had been reluctant to do it because I am not naturally given to making a fool of myself. But it was Bernie's idea so I was prepared to put up with a red face if it was to give her a laugh.

There were a couple of double-takes among the Celtic staff before people realised it was me. The guys in the dressing room loved it. Then Charlie Nicholas told me the gaffer was still in the bath.

Now Tommy Burns is not exactly renowned for having the world's best eyesight. The bath at Parkhead is just behind the door so I casually walked straight past him and into the toilet area. All the boys were hiding behind the door to watch his reactions.

Some swear that as this long-haired vision swept past him, the gaffer squinted to focus on me and rapidly moved his hands to cover his embarrassment!

Bernadette would live for days like that, when she would wait for me to come home and tell her what happened in minute detail: who said what, who laughed loudest, all that sort of stuff.

She even got her sister to buy her stuff out of the Tam

Shepherd's joke shop in Glasgow and would get me to leave garlic-flavoured sweets lying around in the dressing room to see which players might swallow the gag.

I think she liked to laugh and have fun in spite of all the pain I knew she was going through.

Maybe I lapsed into a state of mind where I thought we could go on like this for ever. Sure, it was tough on Bernie with all her unpleasant treatment with all its unpleasant side-effects.

Death never entered my head. Psychologically, I realise now I was shoving it to the back of my mind. I didn't think about it because it wasn't going to happen that day; and then when the next day came and it wasn't likely to happen then either, it became easier to relegate it further and further from reality.

Ours was never a picture of domestic bliss but Bernie did like to fulfil what she saw as her duties as a wife.

I would go off to training in the morning and would come back to the most fabulous meal at lunch-time. It would be so elaborate, I would sit down to eat it, thinking: 'Where the hell did she get this from?'

Whether I liked it or not, I would tell her that it was fantastic and she'd be strutting around her kitchen, proud as punch that she had created some gastronomic delight for her man.

It turns out she would watch the recipe slot on Richard and Judy's TV show in the morning, see what they were cooking that day and then rush out to Presto's to buy the ingredients.

Sometimes things seemed so normal. As long as she could walk and felt up to it, we would go for nights out on the town like any other young couple.

At the same time, my heart would drop if ever we found ourselves in situations where I thought it could damage her already fragile health.

One of those occasions happened when we were on holiday in Gran Canaria during the summer of 1994. I remember being really concerned for her when we went to an Irish bar one night for a good old sing-along. Cancer was by this time into her lungs and this place had a low ceiling and really reeked with a heavy, smoky atmosphere.

But there was no telling Bernie. Everyone in the place was drunk and we were swept along by the good company and the singing.

On other nights there, it was Bernadette who would hate to go back to the hotel. We would be out 'clubbing' until 5 a.m. and she would be telling me off for wanting to crawl back to my bed.

I wanted that holiday to go on forever.

Back in Scotland, we'd eat at our favourite restaurant, Maxaluna in Glasgow's Sauchiehall Street. We'd also like to take in the pictures (as if we hadn't seen enough movies during the night!).

Our companions would inevitably be Bernie's sister, Elizabeth and her Gary, or her bridesmaid Jackie McQuade and her boyfriend, James Gardner.

She would come alive when we were out on the town because it was the scene she knew really well from her days when she managed a pub. By now, she was not too keen on chatting to people because they were saying how sorry they felt for her; but she didn't want to hear all that.

One of the nicest sights I remember was in the Voodoo Room, a night club in Glasgow we went to well into Bernie's chemotherapy and steroid treatment.

I knew she wasn't happy with her appearance; the steroids had piled on the weight and she had a chubby little face, poking out from the bandanna covering her head.

There we were, standing on the edge of the dance floor as the music boomed out. She didn't know I was watching her, but I could see her wee head bobbing along to the sound. Her legs were giving her a lot of pain, I know, but there she was, shuffling on the spot. Aching to be up there with everyone else.

I beamed with pride.

Chapter Thirteen
Christmas by Video

HAND-held video cameras are supposed to be fun items, used for capturing baby's first steps, christenings, holidays and birthdays. Yet when Bernie and I received one as a wedding present from Elizabeth and Gary, I could not have imagined the use to which it would be put just eight months later.

Come Christmas 1994, Bernie was a virtual prisoner in her own bed. She had been trapped there for two months, save for one week in December which she had had to spend in hospital while she underwent radiotherapy. There was hardly a part of her body which cancer had not attacked or was presently attacking.

To maintain a semblance of normality, we invited members of the family to our home for Christmas Day. Bernie's sister, Mary, came with Willie and the two kids. They brought the Christmas present they received from Bernie, a wee Cocker Spaniel puppy called Jasper. It was the first dog in the McStay family for over a hundred years. Irene was there as well.

But because of her condition, Bernie had to lie upstairs in bed while we tucked into turkey and all the trimmings.

I would get the camcorder out and record the table, set out in all its finery. I'd film Mary cutting the turkey in the kitchen and the kids, with their party hats on, getting wolfed into the Christmas dinner. Everyone would record their own little message to Bernie and sign off with a smile or a wave.

Then I would take the machine upstairs and run the tape for Bernie. It meant she was able to share a little in the big day.

Christmas was a time when Bernie would normally be in her element; she would be out on the town with her pals, shopping, dancing and generally living it up. But the wee thing was stuck in her bed now, dependent on me and a Japanese video camera for all of her fun.

Bernie, Elizabeth and I used to have little tea parties, up there in the bed.

Liz would keep her going with all sorts of girlie chat; after I had come back from training I could fill her in with all the gossip about the boys from Celtic. We were her only real communication with the outside world.

Liz or Mary would carry out shopping raids on Tunnocks in Uddingston, bringing in a pile of sausage-rolls and cakes. Some times in the afternoons, with the sun coming into the room, we might all drift off to sleep lying there in the bed.

And maybe because I was seeing her every day, I did not notice any deterioration in her physical condition. I know now she must have changed, but I didn't see it happening. Throughout her hard times, I would do everything in my power to be positive, or more importantly, to appear positive.

There were occasions when she would try to broach the subject of death; how, if the worst came to the worst, what she would want me to do with my life.

But she would only need to start the sentence and I would know where it was going to lead. I'd stop her in her tracks.

'Don't talk like that, darling,' I'd say. 'We've got the next 10 or 20 years together, so don't waste your time talking like that.'

Nevertheless, she did catch me crying a few times on my own and she would try to be strong for me.

What really saddens me is that Bernie would have given anything to be a mother. Even after we discovered she had terminal cancer, we would talk about how we were going to have kids, never mind the fact that we knew we couldn't. Maybe that was us, again, thinking we'd get our miracle.

We would even pick kids' names. We'd sit in bed and ask ourselves: 'Now, what should we call our first-born boy?'

I said: 'What about Maximilian Mowbray? I quite fancy the sound of that.'

Bernie would squeal with delight; as long as it was something outrageous, she would give it qualified approval.

Whether we would have gone for Max or the full Maximilian, I don't know but that's how realistically we took it.

Because we had been to Disney World in Florida and seen the faces of little kids there, we would sit and plan our trip to America. We decided we would wait until our little ones were at least eight years old before taking them there.

Privately, in your own mind, you start asking yourself questions like: 'Why did God not let us meet sooner?' We could have had a family during the period when she was in remission. She loved kids, desperately.

She told Elizabeth that her biggest regret was not being able to leave behind a little bit of her . . . for me to have. A little Max could be sitting on my knee now, even if I didn't have his mummy.

I must admit, I did shed a tear when I saw Ally McCoist and his wife in the paper with their new baby boy in January 1995.

It might seem strange, bearing in mind the fear that we both knew it may have been our last Christmas together, but Bernie and I did not exchange Christmas presents. She was obviously unable to go Christmas shopping, so she insisted that I should not buy anything for her; if she could not give me a Christmas present, she didn't want to receive one from me.

We agreed that we would postpone our Christmas shopping until February, when she would be well enough to get out again.

That was a real pity because she had been saving up for something for six months. I used to come in to the house after training with Celtic and dump all of my loose change on the kitchen worktop. The little Magpie had assembled £500, which she intended splashing out on me at Christmas.

The money is still in her purse beside the bed. Maybe I will

127

go out in the next few months and buy that Christmas gift from Bernie.

She was well enough on Christmas Day to sit up and watch my efforts on the video recorder. She even persuaded me to join up with my Celtic team-mates for the Boxing Day match at Aberdeen.

I drove up to Aberdeen on the morning of the game with Willie McStay and Bernie's dad. I was really thrilled, when I called her on the car phone on the way home, to hear how chirpy she sounded; this was a girl who seemed ready for a good night out. She had been listening to the game on the radio and she told me off for getting booked at Pittodrie.

I remember turning to Bernie's dad in the car and saying: 'It's great, Jimmy, she sounds fantastic.'

When we got home, she was crashed out. Absolutely shattered. And that's when I first realised things were beginning to slip away from me.

By now, she was hooked up to a syringe driver, a little device that pumps a constant stream of morphine into the body to combat the pain. I think that it was the high concentration of morphine that was making her sleep all of the time, but even in that state she was full of surprises.

Her friend Jackie and her sister came in to see her at one point, when she appeared to be sleeping. When Jackie touched Bernie's hand, she almost sat up and practically jumped out of the bed.

'Ooh, hi, Jackie,' she said, 'It's great to see you.'

Then, seconds later, she'd fall back on to the covers and she'd be asleep again. I was really pleased for Jackie that she had that communication with her friend in the days before she died.

The pain and discomfort which Bernadette was experiencing was really awful. When she did come round, I would try to coax her back into unconsciousness. 'Go back to sleep, darling,' I would whisper because I knew that it was best for her.

Her mouth was blistered and ulcerated. She hadn't had much to drink for two weeks because she could hardly keep anything down. Her lips were so dry, they seemed to be sticking together.

Eventually, I got little Sun lollies which are made of soft ice, rather than the hard ones. We would rub these across her lips to keep them as moist as we could and she started to take them in.

In her last few days, she must have had about 50 Sun lollies.

It seemed like a different world, up in our bedroom. You were barely aware of people coming and going in that world downstairs but you were keenly aware of everything in our own little world.

Towards the end, you just don't want to leave your wife's side. I ached to be close to her but if I got too close, it would mean more pain and discomfort for her.

So I would lie on the bed beside her, keeping an eye on her breathing which had been a bit erratic. She would either be breathing very, very heavily and slowly or breathing in little bursts, then nothing for around 15 seconds.

I just couldn't sleep at night, because you are forever on edge, waiting for her to breathe properly. I suppose the parents of new-born babies may understand what it's like.

But even in that world where she was spending most of her time now, she was still able to slip back to give me some lovely, tender moments which showed our love was still alive.

As she slept, I would lean over and ask her for a kiss. She was definitely not awake yet she was somehow able to raise her head ever so slightly and pout her lips towards me.

I would be telling her that I love her and you would see her lips move, but nothing would come out. I know that was her trying to tell me: 'I love you, too, Mog.'

At this time, the rest of the world was celebrating the arrival of the New Year 1995. Hogmanay came and went with no more fuss than the ticking of the clock. Up in our world, I was holding on to the last moment's of my wife's life. In those circumstances, what did it matter if the clock struck twelve?

Every minute was split into precious moments. These are moments that will stay with me for ever; even in her last hour, she managed to give me a kiss.

In the last half-hour of her life, it was obvious that the pain had all left her. She could half turn on her side towards me, something she hadn't been able to do because it hurt so badly, and she would cuddle into me. I would talk to her, profess my undying love for her and tell her how proud I was that she was my wife. She was practically lying on my chest when she passed away; her breathing gradually becoming softer and softer and in an instant, I knew she was gone.

The colour just drained from her and her lovely eyes turned black. As I held her in my arms, I nuzzled my head into her ear and told her: 'I will do you proud, darling.'

Through my tears, I gave her my final promise. I told her that in all that I do in my life from now on, I will succeed for her. Whether it is on the park or in football management or in any other capacity, she will be proud of me.

Nothing made her happier than seeing me in the papers, my big ugly mug sticking out from somewhere in the sports pages. That is just a sign of love – wanting your partner to do well in whatever field they have chosen. So if that's what I knew gave her pleasure, I know it will please her if I maintain that success.

On her Christmas card to Dr Bissett, Bernadette had written: 'Thanks for all your fine treatment in 1994. Hope it carries on in '95.'

In fact, she lived for just 14 hours of the New Year, passing away at 2.15 p.m.

I wouldn't let her go. Everyone who came into the room wanted to touch her but you were almost afraid to let her slip from your grasp. As if that was somehow final.

Strangely, my tears lasted just 15 minutes that day. All the girls were crying their eyes out and I just thought I had to be strong for them. I gained an inner strength from somewhere. I don't know where it came from or why it happened because I am a sensitive type of guy. But it just seemed there was so much heartache among people who were close to Bernadette that someone had to give them a shoulder. And I decided it would be me.

Within a quarter of an hour of Bernadette's death, I had thrown myself into arrangements for her funeral, based on the same principles on which I had organised our wedding the year before: nothing but the best for Bernie.

She deserved the best. So I must have somehow switched on to 'automatic pilot' and channelled all of my emotions and energies into organising a farewell fitting for my wife. It was as if she was still upstairs and I was making myself busy downstairs, organising a birthday party for Bernie.

We set about finding the best of everything. If the cars at a funeral director's were not the newest or the shiniest, they were rejected out of hand.

When it came to picking a coffin, I found it hard to get my wishes over to the company. I didn't want just an ordinary coffin. The thing that would take my Bernadette on her final journey would have to be something special.

I wasn't doing it for show, though I knew the funeral would be conducted under the full glare of the media spotlight. It was simply that my wife deserved something big and strong, where she'd be safe from any harm.

The thing that stuck in my mind was the funeral of the American President, John F. Kennedy. Although I was only born the day he died, I have seen numerous black and white newsreels of the final procession to Arlington Cemetery.If he could have a casket fit for a king, there was no reason why my Bernie could not have a similar one, fit for a queen.

Eventually, I convinced the undertaker that in my choice of coffin, cost was not to be a consideration. He showed me a brochure from Cathedral Caskets in London and I knew right away the one I wanted.

It was big and bronze with large, gold handles. It stood out. Despite the fact that things were more difficult to arrange because of the New Year holiday, everything worked out fine in the end. It so happened that there was one in stock; yes, they would be able to transport it north in time.

I slept beside Bernadette in the bed on the night after she died. From time to time, I would wake and stretch out my hand to touch her. We had Masses for her every night after that until it came time to close the coffin.

She was dwarfed by the sheer scale of it. But I didn't mind, because it made her seem so safe.

On the night of Thursday, January 5, Bernadette's body was due to be taken to the church, where it would lie overnight, in keeping with traditional Catholic funerals.

I remember the undertaker allowing me to seal the coffin by turning the nuts with a little golden spanner, which I've kept. I remember walking the hearse out of our estate in Bothwell, which I think Bernie would have liked.

To be honest, the events of the next day are something of a blur to me. There was an unreal atmosphere in the house because the place was full of people; family who had come up from England for the funeral and friends you hadn't seen in ages. The house was so chock-full of folk that it actually reminded me of my wedding day.

Therefore, with so many people around me, there wasn't really any way I could slip into a state of unrestrained grief. I got through the night before alright, considering it was my first night without Bernie beside me. I got up, washed and shaved as normal and was conscious of trying to ensure I looked my best for the big day ahead.

To make sure the close family arrived as one at the church, we arranged for everyone to go to the Glynhill Hotel in Paisley beforehand, where they could take their seats in the official cars.

I knew the Press and TV would be waiting at the church, but honestly it was not something which was preoccupying my thoughts. Radio Clyde had asked permission to place a microphone inside the church to record the Mass but I knew that if we had agreed to that, BBC Scotland would want a camera team in and we could then end up with an unseemly scramble with sound men falling over photographers.

Celtic's public relations manager Peter McLean had been very helpful, acting as a liaison between the family and the Press. He issued a request for privacy and asked newspapers to publicise our wish that flowers should not be sent. We asked people who felt moved to do something, to send a donation to the Beatson Institute instead.

You don't mind the media actually being there. You realise that there is a certain amount of public interest in what happened to me and Bernie. The only line I would draw under their involvement is that their presence does not become intrusive, and fortunately that did not happen.

People say I handled myself well at the funeral itself, at St John's R.C. Church in the Renfrewshire town of Barrhead, where Bernie grew up. I didn't feel particularly under pressure or worried that I might break down at any moment. But the truth is, I was completely numb.

I had been to funerals before and I remembered looking at the people in the front row and thinking to myself: 'God, how do they manage to get through this?'

You usually notice it's the ladies who seem physically less able to cope with the trauma of it all. I can honestly remember wondering if I would one day be sat there on the front row and pondering how I would be able to handle it.

And there, on 6 January 1995, I was sat in that very spot. And I was discovering exactly how I would feel. Numb. Cold. Detached. Not feeling a thing.

The Mass itself went straight over my head, much to my regret now. Sad as the day was, I would still like to have some memories of things that were said.

Little things stick out. I remember Father O'Keeffe, who had married us in Paisley, describing to the 1200 mourners 'a marvellous girl'.

He added: 'Despite what she was going through, she was always more concerned about how everyone else was.

'Her father always told me Bernie was special. She never grumbled or complained once.'

The card on my flowers to her contained deliberate echoes of our wedding and of her promise to sit on my shoulder in my life ahead. Just as our rings proclaimed our 'eternal love' to each other, so too did my final message. It read: 'To my guardian angel. Our eternal love laughs in the face of death. Together, forever, Mog and Bern.'

The club was well represented. Chief executive Fergus McCann was there, along with Tommy Burns and Billy Stark and among the players were Paul McStay, Paddie Bonner, John Collins, Charlie Nicholas and poor Andy Walker, whose father had died just a few months before. Even 'Pally' made it up from Manchester.

When the soloist sang the haunting hymn 'On Eagles Wings', with its chorus 'And I will raise you up, on eagles' wings', I felt the first rush of emotion I had experienced that day. I was suddenly aware of a huge lump in my throat, fighting to get out.

But it was at the graveside that the feelings threatened to overwhelm me. The grave might not look so bad from a distance, with the green artificial grass neatly covering the earth.

But stood there, peering into this gaping hole in the ground, I could not believe that this is where my Bernie would end up.

I would not say my good-byes here; not with all these people around; not as her coffin's being lowered into this hole in the ground. The worms were squirming around in the muck. I had to catch myself from feeling faint.

I had said my good-bye in the house, just the two of us. And if our belief is right, all we were lowering into this hole was a body. Bernie's spirit had already left . . . and was sitting right there on my shoulder.

It would not be long before I was to discover if my heavenly protector had started fighting my corner. We had the usual reception afterwards at the Glynhill Hotel, the place we had started out from that morning. But it was on the way home that the full impact of the day hit me . . . in dramatic fashion.

I was in my car with my dad, just coming off the M73 at Calderpark Zoo and edging on to the M74 Carlisle Road. I just fell asleep at the wheel.

My car swerved into the next lane, colliding with a van travelling in the same direction and only the quick-thinking of my dad prevented a tragedy. He dived across me to grab the steering wheel and dragged the car back into its proper lane.

I can only think that I had been in such a high state of mental awareness for most of the funeral, my guard must have slipped at that vital time. Maybe I was just exhausted.

But I recall, in a hazy sort of way, my eyes beginning to close just as we began to round that bend and the natural curve of the road pulling us into the van's path. If it had been a juggernaut, we would have been under the wheels and smashed to pieces.

We stopped on the hard shoulder a bit further down the motorway to see just how bad the damage had been. The van driver recognised me and was really decent about it all.

Maybe he knew I had been on my way back from my wife's funeral, I'm not sure, but he said the damage to his van wasn't worth bothering about and headed off.

Later, I was in two minds about Bernie's involvement in the crash. On one hand, I thought: 'That just shows my Guardian

Angel is looking after me.'

And then I asked myself: 'Could that have been Bernie, willing me to join her in heaven?'

Chapter Fourteen
Captain of Celtic

I HAD been a Celtic player for almost three-and-a-half years when Celtic manager Tommy Burns appointed me captain for the first time.

It was the Scottish Cup clash with Meadowbank Thistle in February 1995, during the period Paul McStay had failed to earn a first-team place.

Tommy goes around all the players before a game, encouraging them to do well and pointing out their particular responsibilities.

It was my first game back after Bernadette's death at New Year. When Tommy came to me, he told me to 'keep things tight' then added: 'You take them out today, Mogga.'

I was thrilled. I was an Englishman playing my football in Scotland and here was I, being asked to captain a club like Celtic.

It was a fantastic honour, repeated the following week for the Premier League game with Hearts at Tynecastle.

Being captain makes you concentrate even more on your game than you would normally. If you are up against a six-foot attacker, you tell yourself that you are going to win everything in the air. But as well as focusing on your own game, you are also required to organise and gee-up your team-mates as well. It's vital not to let the game go stale or allow players to go to sleep.

For someone who captained Middlesbrough for the best part of a decade, I have found it difficult to assert my personality on my fellow team-mates at Celtic.

After all, this is a dressing room full of established international players, like Paul McStay, John Collins and Packie

Bonner. They know what Celtic is all about. It's not like any other club, because it has this special history and tradition to be proud of.

For me, an outsider, to come in and stamp my total personality on this special club was never really on. How could I be top dog at Celtic Park? I had never even heard that they won the European Cup in 1967...and I had been trained at Ayresome Park by former Celtic legend Bobby Murdoch!

But having to leave that aspect of my play behind became a growing disappointment to me. I'm the type of person who thrives on being given responsibility; I can feel myself grow in stature when I have people looking towards me for guidance, encouragement, leadership. But while Paul is there, the captaincy is not really an issue. Everyone can see the reasoning for Paul McStay being captain. Believe me, the players desperately want to win something – not just for themselves but especially for Paul.

Having said that, I still feel that if I had not suffered such bad injuries in my first year at Celtic, I would now be a much more dominant force at the club. I have no doubt about my ability when I am fit and my life is on an even keel and I am happy with myself.

Tommy Burns now explains his thinking behind making me captain:

'I just wanted to mark, in some way, Tony's return to the team after the death of his wife. It was almost throwing down a gauntlet before him, offering him the responsibility of captaining Celtic and urging him to take it.

'I may be a football manager, but I am also a man. I knew that there were leadership qualities in Tony's personality but, more importantly, I realised that after the death of Bernadette, there were all sorts of emotions churning around in his head and in his heart.

'I knew it was possible that we might be able to channel those energies in a positive way; to give him an aim in life, something to really focus on. If handing him the Celtic captain's armband in some way helped to do that, then of course I would offer it to him. It just happened to coincide with a spell where our regular captain, Paul McStay, was not featuring in the team. I concede it was psychology, designed to try and lift him out of himself in much the same way as when we asked him to warm up the boys before training.

'We were saying to him: 'You are an important part of this team; show us just how important you can be.'

'It gave him something to focus on, to think about and occupy some mental time during a period when his thoughts might stray to the tragedy which had nearly swept him away from us. It brought him back and I am delighted with the way he responded to that challenge.

'When I became the manager of Celtic, I looked for this tough, big guy who had come north with this amazing reputation as a battler, a true leader on the park who would play with his heart on his sleeve.

'What I found was a quiet, almost secluded character who was hardly ever at the ground. He would no sooner finish training but he would be off home again. We decided he was not what we were looking for.

'We had tried to be as fair as we possibly could. We had told Tony that his wife had to be his number one priority; if he had to be with her, we perfectly understood.

'But at the same time, we had a football club to turn around. This game can be terribly unforgiving. Would anyone have said at the end of the season: 'Well, we know Celtic finished fifth in the league but we accept that, because Tony Mowbray was out for the bulk of the season?' No, I don't think people would have said that, either.

'To be perfectly honest, we were looking for someone to replace him. We looked at him in training and we looked at him

139

in the games when he was able to appear. There were times when he was so remote I actually thought he was trying to wind me up; I would be trying to have little team-talks and I would see big Tony staring into space, gazing into another world.

'Only later, when I would think about it, did I realise he had more important things on his mind. It was obvious that his wife was getting the best of him and Celtic Football Club was getting the remains. But since Bernadette's death, he has come back a new man and made that position his own. Where before we were only getting a bit of him, now we are getting all of him. The transformation in the man has been incredible. Perhaps it is the result of this enormous weight being lifted from his shoulders, but whatever the reason, we are all thrilled that he has come through the experience in such positive fashion.

'He has played five games now since his return and he's been our best man on each occasion.

'The measure of his performance and determination when leading from the front in those two games has to raise the possibility that he is a Celtic captain in the making.

'We are trying to transform Celtic from an unsuccessful football club to a successful one. It is not easy.

'But it means we have to look at every aspect of our game. I know Paul McStay has been club captain for many years now but it is not written in stone that Paul McStay will be captain for ever.

'The prospect also exists that I will bring in someone who I believe will be an even more suitable captain than Tony Mowbray.

'And it's not just on the park that his influence on the club is being felt . When we travelled to Spain to play Real Madrid in February, it was big Tony who was organising the quiz among the players in the hotel.

'A lot of people operate to a set of values which dictate that a man's man is someone who ducks and dives, who takes shortcuts and takes a good drink.

'Tony Mowbray does none of those things; but to my way of thinking, Tony Mowbray is a man in the true sense of the word.

'He stands for every good and decent principle there is; he conducts himself in a way we all can learn from; the way he loved his wife and showed true support for her family. Absolutely incredible.

'If the young players at Celtic are wise enough, they will look to Tony Mowbray as a role model for how to lead their life. To some, the lesson could go right over their head but they are very lucky to have a person of Tony's integrity to learn from.'

Chapter Fifteen
Picking Up The Pieces

THE first words I utter when I get out of bed each day are: 'Good morning, darling.' And last thing at night, when I close the bedroom door, it is again my wife who occupies my thoughts and my words.

I talk to her all day, every day, whether I am in the house or driving in my car. But that is not to say that Tony Mowbray has failed to turn his back on tragedy.

What happened to Bernadette could not be undone, I fully realise that. But in the pain and heartache of losing my wife, I understand that I have a duty to myself to rebuild my life.

Tommy Burns' decision to make me captain helped me concentrate my thoughts on football. It gave me responsibility I had not felt at Celtic before; that it was me who was leading the team out and it was to me that other players were looking for example.

In that sense, I feel lucky that I have a football club I can steep myself in whenever my private thoughts threaten to engulf me.

The importance of family involvement cannot be overstated either. My mam, who lives down south, stayed with me for six weeks after the death of Bernadette; Elizabeth has been around me all the time; I went to see the Oscar-winning movie Forrest Gump the other night with Irene; and Patrick, Bernie's brother, bought me a classical guitar so that he can teach me one or two songs.

I get the very distinct impression that Bernadette had spoken to them all, making it her last request that I am not allowed to be left on my own for any length of time.

But being involved with a club like Celtic is so multi-dimensional that it means someone in my circumstances can dip in and out of whatever aspect of the club I like.

For example, Tommy Burns called me in one day in January to say that he had agreed to let some breast cancer campaigners come to the ground to get more publicity for their efforts by being photographed with some of the players.

The press conference was happening that day and Tommy was well aware it was still a very sensitive time for me. He said it was basically up to me whether I wanted to go along or not.

I told him I would quite happily pose for pictures with the rest of the squad, but that I did not feel comfortable being interviewed by any journalists. Once you give some reporters an inch, they will take the proverbial mile.

Publicity pictures were taken by the various photographers called to Celtic Park, and Audrey Jones, of the Scottish Breast Cancer Campaign, asked me if she could have a quiet chat with me in the corner. She's a nice lady, and she outlined for me what the campaign was all about how the disease is the second-biggest killer of women in this country and; how most of the money raised for breast cancer research came from donations or charitable fund-raising events.

Despite my own personal involvement, I had not realised that the Government had allowed such a situation to develop. I was appalled. If breast cancer is such a big killer of women, why are more public funds not devoted to finding a cure for it?

It seems so unfair, particularly since so much is known about the number-one killer, heart disease. Not only do we have a great deal of knowledge about heart disease, but millions of pounds are spent warning people that they increase their chances of developing problems if they eat carelessly, smoke heavily or fail to take sufficient exercise.

But what do we know about the root causes of cancer? Is it something that is determined by lifestyle? Is it hereditary? Who knows?

Almost 30,000 British women are diagnosed with breast

cancer every year. Statistically, every woman in the country has a one-in-twelve chance of suffering from it at some stage in her life. It kills 16,000 women every year.

Should we not be asking why our mortality rate is the highest in the western world?

Even when it is diagnosed, breast cancer treatment in this country is so haphazard that your chances of survival can depend on where you live.

No wonder it is called a lottery.

It is now considered vital that a woman with breast cancer should be treated by a specialist unit. Yet, until February of this year, there was no all-encompassing guide to specialist breast care services in Britain. So when women suffering from breast cancer were referred by their GPs, they were often referred to general surgeons, rather than to the experts in the field.

When a guide to specialist services was published earlier this year, it was typically the Cancer Relief Macmillan Fund who produced it – a charity. Professor Roger Blamey, of Nottingham City Hospital and chairman of the British Association of Surgical Oncology, said at the time of the guide's launch that the current levels of treatment for breast cancer in this country are 'very variable'.

He added: 'There is a very wide gulf between the best and worst practice in the diagnosis and management of breast cancer in this country.

'A woman referred to a general surgeon may have to wait three months for an appointment. She may be seen several times by junior staff who can't make up their minds and she may be poorly advised about the treatments available to her. That's a terrible situation.'

I agree. I also agreed with Audrey that day at Parkhead to support the Scottish Breast Cancer Campaign further by taking a 200,000-name petition to 10 Downing Street.

We travelled down to London the week after the initial press conference at Celtic. Of course, it wasn't John Major who accepted the petition at the front door of No.10 but it did give the campaigners a photo opportunity as it was handed over to a member of his staff.

I am sure it would be so easy for me to slip into the role of Tony Mowbray, breast cancer campaigner. If I was looking for a seat on various committees, I am positive that they would be made available to me.

But I decided I had to get back into my football and channel my energies into getting Celtic back on the winning path again. I needed to pick up the pieces of the only job I had ever known.

In any case, why should I have to campaign for decent medical care for women? My God, we pay enough in Income Tax and National Insurance to expect a standard of treatment befitting a major economic power like Britain.

Just because I am not taking up the cause full-time does not mean that I cannot get the message over in my own way – and again, that is the beauty of belonging to a club like Celtic.

The first Celtic Supporters Club function I attended after the death of Bernadette provided the perfect opportunity to let people know about Britain's shameful breast cancer record. It was at Livingston, West Lothian, and the night had been going so well. I was cruising; I had been playing pool with a lot of the fans, and you can tell how people who support the club are always so grateful when a player goes along to their events.

Just moments before I was due to speak, I had been talking to the supporters club chairman, a chap sitting next to me and I felt perfectly OK.

I got up to say a few words and as soon as I mentioned my thanks for the £1500 they had raised for cancer research, I became gripped with tension.

From feeling totally relaxed one minute, the mention of Bernadette's name just took my breath away. I started sweating and tingling and I could hear my voice beginning to break. You

145

do try to say to yourself: 'Now, come on, get a grip, man.' I didn't actually cry but I had to ask the audience to excuse me for a minute while I regained my composure.

Already there are a few Player of the Year invitations coming through, at which I will be expected to speak again. Hopefully, the difficulty will ease with each passing event.

And then, the other day, I received a lovely letter from a 13-year-old girl from Edinburgh, Susan McCann. She told me how she had read about Bernie in *The Sunday Mail* and then watched a special Oprah Winfrey programme about breast cancer on TV.She felt compelled to write to me, to ask what she could do to help. She's a season ticket holder with Celtic but I arranged for her and her dad to come along to the tea-room after our league game with Motherwell in April and have a chat. I gave her an autographed ball, which she can take back to her school and raffle for a breast cancer charity. I told her not to set any targets for herself over how much money she should raise; if she took in £5 then that was £5 more that could be used to find a cure.

Some school friends of Bernadette's organised a disco in The Columba Club in Barrhead around the same time, raising the amazing sum of £3000. And young players like Simon Donnelly are coming into the ground all the time with cheques they have been given as a result of fund-raising events.

But is it not remarkable that ordinary people, including a young girl just into her teens, should feel moved to push back the frontiers of medical knowledge? And the Government, our leaders who should be showing us the way, don't seem to be bothered.I would honestly love to see our politicians sit in the waiting room of a cancer clinic for just one day of their very busy lives. To be honest, that's a daft suggestion because they would just get in the way.

Bob Wilson, the former Scotland goalkeeper-turned-broadcaster, wrote recently about his experiences in hospital when he took his daughter, Anna, for radiotherapy treatment.

He hit it right on the nose when he described the 160 seats in the waiting area, each one of them occupied by a cancer sufferer. And those 160 seats were occupied every day the Wilsons went for treatment.

It was so true: it reminded me of the times Bernie and I would go to hospital and the clinics would be mobbed-out with so many people, there simply would not be enough room for everyone.

The nurses and junior doctors would be rushed off their feet, yet they somehow feel able to build up relationships with people they know may not live very much longer. I honestly don't know how they can do that.

And the courage of the cancer patients themselves. It was a lesson to me to see how people, knowing what they had, regularly attending hospital and cheerily passing the time of day with people lying in the next bed to them.

Perhaps it is only natural for politicians to demonstrate the same ambivalence to breast cancer as many other people show; if it has not affected them, it simply doesn't happen. And I suppose there is also a strong call for cash to be directed towards diseases involving children.

But once you are in that ditch and you are attending hospital for treatment, everyone in your sphere is affected by cancer and it seems somehow so much more real.

Then, it's not just a woman's disease. It affects the husband, or the brother or the son.

I know only too well of the way whole families can be devastated by a death, through the many letters I received in the weeks and months after Bernie passed away.

People who have already lost someone seem to have a greater grasp of life than those who have still to experience a loss; it's as if they have stepped forward to peer over the cliff-edge and stepped back to a place of safety.

I don't know how people can find it within themselves to

write to a total stranger and tell him of their most intimate and loving moments, but I'm glad they did.

Letters literally came in by the hundred, people even writing poems and songs to get their caring message across to me.

I was stunned by one letter from two girls, who said they were impressed by the way I had stood by my wife throughout her difficulties. What stunned me was the belief that this was somehow unusual; who wouldn't stand by their wife?

Most were just keen to offer words of comfort; to explain to me how their experience has shown that the passing of time will heal the pain.

One supporter wrote a poem to me, called 'The Hard Man':

'Forget your Johnny Stark
Forget your razor Ben
Here's to Tony Mowbray
A chief among hard men.

'Tony came from Middlesbrough to Celtic
At first his play got pelted
But when the big man was in Bernie's arms
His massive heart just melted.

'Any player joining Celtic
Is put through a rigorous test
And like everything Tony tackles in life
He gave of his very best.

'Tony would show plenty of character
in later months
When Bernadette took ill
This is when the hard man came to the fore

And showed great strength of will.
'Tony and Bernie got married at the altar
Their unquestioned love they vowed
Knowing they wouldn't have long together
Their love stood tall and unbowed.
 'Tony cared for Bernie
While playing for his club
Any other so-called hard man
Would be drowning his sorrows in the pub.

'Nine months later, Tony buried Bernie
His brave and beautiful wife
Many a man would have slumped in a heap
After losing the love of his life.

'So let's get things into perspective
Instead of moaning about a defeat by Raith
We must all now be humbled
After witnessing Tony's great faith.

'That's what you call a really hard man
Who with dignity can handle all that grief
So let's all pray, in the months ahead
Tony will get some relief.'

On the day of Bernadette's funeral, I received an astonishing letter from a man in Wales. It read:
Dear Tony,
          My darling wife died a week ago, 27 December, after a long fight against cancer, aged 51.

The funeral service is this afternoon, but I felt that a few words from me to you will help, in some small way, for you to take strength knowing that a tremendous number of people are sharing your grief.

In the hundreds of letters and cards of condolence that I have received, many have written that 'words are so inadequate' but I have found so much strength, knowing that Jan, my wife, was so loved by so many who took the time to write. I am sure this is the case with your lovely Bernadette.

Please, God, that a cure for cancer is found in the very near future to stop the dreadful suffering that our lovely wives and others have had to endure.

My prayers and thoughts are with you,

G.L.

There were others; so many thoughtful people.

Dear Tony,

I just thought I would drop you a note to express my sincere sadness in hearing of the passing away of your wife, Bernadette.

I know the unbearable pain you are going through at the moment but I am sure your wife would have wanted you to be strong at this time.

I lost my wife in a car crash in August of 1993. We had only been married for 14 months. At the time, I felt as if my whole world had ended but with the help of my family and friends, I managed to get through the really bad times and only now do I really feel as if I have finally come to terms with what has happened.

Tony, I know we do not know each other although I have seen you many times at Parkhead and I hope you do not consider this letter an intrusion into your grief. But I really found my family and friends to be of great comfort to me. Perhaps you may find this, too.

Yours Sincerely, J.A.

Dear Tony,

I have just read about your wife's sad demise and would like to offer my sincere condolences.

I, too, lost my wife to cancer seven years ago, when we were both only 21. We were only married for three days when she died and I know no amount of words will ever heal the pain of the loss you have endured.

I can only hope that with the help of both families, and Celtic Football Club, the team my wife and I supported, you will overcome this terrible event in your life.

My thoughts will be with you over the coming months. Again, may I say how sorry I am about your wife. She was a beautiful woman with a lot to live for,

Yours Sincerely, A.H.

Dear Tony,

I would like to offer you my sincere condolences on the loss of your wife, Bernadette.

Knowing how you are feeling. I went through the same thing myself, when I lost my wife in 1993. I was informed by a specialist that she had cancer and told that she would have between six and 12 months to live. My two children, a boy and a girl, decided with me that it was best not to tell my wife.

We had just returned from Cyprus after a two-week holiday, in September 1992, when the diagnosis came through. My wife passed away in my arms as we sat on the end of the bed.

Tony, I hope you don't mind me writing this letter but I just felt that I had to, knowing how you must be feeling. One thing you will always have is your memories.

Once again, my deepest sympathy to you and your family,

Yours Sincerely, A.R.

Dear Tony,

I was so sad to read in the newspapers that you have recently lost your wife. Please accept my sincere condolences on your tragic loss.

I know how you are feeling, as I lost my wife to the same disease in December 1994.

She was only 39 and was diagnosed as having cancer of the bowel in June last year. She fought bravely, but unfortunately, to no avail.

As with you and Bernadette, we had everything to look forward to. I am a company director, the business is doing very well, we have two lovely children (a four-year-old girl and a boy of 11) a nice house etc etc but unfortunately, this mother of all diseases has no scruples over who it attacks.

Let's both hope that someone, somewhere, sooner rather than later can come up with a cure so that future generations do not have to go through what you and I are experiencing now.

The main reason I wrote is that I wanted you to read the attached verse. It was in a card I received from a friend.

I was also at my wife's side when the end came and she died very peacefully. Among the last words she ever spoke to me were 'Oh, darling. I am so happy.'

The words in the verse reflect how my wife felt right at the end and I hope you can glean as much comfort from them as I have done,

Best wishes for the future, TT.

Death is nothing at all.....I have only slipped away into the next room

I am I and you are you . . . whatever we were to each other
that we still are
Call me by my old familiar name. Speak to me in the easy
way you always used
Put no difference in your tone. Wear no forced air of
solemnity or sorrow
Laugh as we always laughed at the little jokes we enjoyed
together
Play, smile, think of me, pray for me
Let my name be ever the household word
that it always had been
Let it be spoken without effect, without the ghost of a shadow
on it
Life means all that it ever meant
It is the same that it ever was
There is absolutely unbroken continuity
Why should I be out of mind
Because I am out of sight?
I am just waiting for you
Somewhere very near, just around the corner
All is well

Henry Scott Holland (1847-1910)

Particularly touching were letters I received from Rangers
supporters.

Dear Tony Mowbray,

I am a Rangers supporter and was saddened

to hear of your loss. I saw photographs of your wife, Bernadette, and I thought she was lovely. I know you will be feeling very sad and I wanted you to know that people are thinking about you.

I wish you well for the future,

Love from Roddy, aged 10.

Another one read:

Dear Tony,

It was with great sadness that I read of your dear wife's death.

I have been a Rangers fan since I was old enough to speak and the club really mean a lot to me.

But may I take this opportunity to offer my sincere condolences to all concerned, especially your good self. My deepest sympathies

God Bless, DD

Dear Tony,

Although I have been a Rangers supporter for 35 years, I feel that I must convey my sincere condolences to you on the tragic death of your wife.

Eight years ago, my brother died at the age of 36 and it seemed like the end of the world to me.

Though this must be a desperately sad time for you, I can tell you that time is indeed a great healer and I hope that you can draw comfort from the fact that the thoughts and sympathies of people from right across the spectrum of Scottish football are with you,

Yours Sincerely

S.M.

One of my greatest regrets, however, is that I have been unable to reply to every one of the letters which came flooding in.

154

The reason for that is simple. While I felt capable of reading them at the time of my bereavement, I have simply not been able to return to them, in this period of recovery, because I know that I will be deeply upset by each and every one.

Maybe in a year or so, people will get a letter out-of-the-blue from Tony Mowbray, thanking them for their kind words of last winter.

Much of my attention recently has been taken up with ensuring that Bernie receives a headstone fitting for my guardian angel. It will have a granite base with 'Bernie' inscribed on it in gold letters. We chose that over 'Mowbray' or 'Doyle' because that was what she loved to be called by everyone.

Then there will be a four-foot plinth with a five-foot guardian angel on top, hewn out of white Italian marble. The plinth is Emerald Pearl, which is coloured black with a fleck of emerald green through it.

Again, it continues the theme we started when we had an emerald set in our engagement rings to show that, when we pledged ourselves to each other, I was playing in Glasgow for Celtic.

There must be a little man in an Italian back street, chipping away at a lump of marble right now. It's the best you can buy. And a picture of Bernie, taken at the time of our engagement, will be super-imposed on to a porcelain plaque at the top.

The inscription will read:

'Bernadette Mowbray. To know her was to love her. Heaven's beauty was enhanced on New Year's Day 1995 when my beautiful wife was taken by the Lord, aged 26.

'Eternal love we shared together our hearts, my darling, entwined forever.' Funnily enough, the object of my adulation would be furious at the amount of money I am spending on her. Bernadette was always very conscious about spending 'our' money on simple household things.

I remember preparing for a holiday and sending her off to buy a couple of beach towels. She got a mouthful from me when she came back with two What Everyone Wants jobs at £1.99 a pair.

Quite what she would say about the expenditure on her headstone, I shudder to think.

But believe me, she is worth it.

Chapter Sixteen
Singing the Same Songs

THE vocal backing of the Celtic support seemed to get louder and louder as the months wore on. Their response to news of Bernie's illness was immediate. 'One Tony Mowbray, There's Only One Tony Mowbray' would come the chant from all ends of the ground.

They could not have known the strength which that gave me through some very difficult times in my life.

The events at Tannadice on April 2 1994, when I scored at Dundee United on the day before my wedding, could almost have come from a scriptwriter.

Celtic fans were located around the tunnel area and they gave me huge roars of support at half-time. Then, when the game was over, they got off their seats and almost to a man gave me a standing ovation. It was my wedding present from them.

Perhaps really top-class players get used to that sort of treatment; fans are always ready to give their heroes a shout of encouragement. But I have never come into the category of 'idol' as a footballer, so this new-found favour with the fans was something unusual for me.

As it happened, Celtic were playing Dundee United again the day after Bernadette's funeral. If I was touched by the vocal support at Tannadice, then I was similarly moved by the same fans' silence at Hampden. The one-minute tribute to Bernadette before the game was universally respected and I am grateful for that.

I have already indicated my total ignorance of all things Celtic before I arrived at the club; indeed I had admitted that I was so ambivalent to the Great Glasgow Divide that I would have been ready to sign for Rangers in 1991.

But this is now 1995 and things are different. Having played for one half of the Old Firm, I would not invite unwanted hostility into my life by signing for 'the other side'.

In any case, there was something about the passion of the Celtic support which gradually led me to believe that there was something more to this club than mere football.

I was steadily being seduced by the devotion of the club's following; by the sheer romance of the green and the white. The feeling of togetherness which Celtic fans seem able to create must stem from the club's roots, which I discovered were anchored in Ireland and the poor east end of Glasgow. Celtic had been founded by a priest, Brother Walfrid, who tried to help feed the needy of the area with cash generated through soccer. This, I was beginning to understand, was no ordinary football club.

I really had my eyes opened on the occasions when Celtic would travel to Ireland for pre-season friendly games or tournaments involving guest clubs from England.

If I had my eyes opened, then the reaction of clubs like Sheffield Wednesday must have been something to behold. We would troop out of the tunnel in a stadium in Dublin and the entire ground would be jam-packed with Celtic supporters waving green-and-white flags.

And you could only imagine that somewhere, perhaps on the second-back row of one of the stands there would be these two Sheffield Wednesday fans who follow their club everywhere looking at each other and wondering 'What country are we in?'

Appearances in Dublin would, effectively, be home games for Celtic. The reception could not be any warmer if we had run out at Celtic Park.

The fans would be waiting to get your autograph at your Dublin hotel and they would be waving to you on your way to the airport.

Suddenly, I was starting to appreciate the feeling of being 'as one' with the fans. When they shouted your name at Parkhead, you were determined to do well for them.....not to let them down.

The people of Middlesbrough still talk about the weekend of my testimonial game in 1992, when the town was 'invaded' by thousands of Celtic fans.

Quite simply, they had never seen anything like it. I remember trying to impress on the people at Ayresome Park that there would be a large travelling support from Scotland.

Because it was a Sunday morning, with an 11 a.m. kick-off, Middlesbrough reckoned they would allocate Celtic 1,000 tickets and stick the supporters in one little corner of the ground.

I was trying to get over to them that they did not have a grasp of what Celtic is all about. I tried to explain that they are the number one choice of opposition among British players who are lucky enough to have a testimonial game.

'Look,' I said, 'they can go to Old Trafford on a Wednesday night and take 20,000 fans along.' Eventually Celtic's security man, George Douglas, travelled down and backed up what I had been saying.

That weekend, more than 11,000 Celtic fans were packed in the area behind one of the goals and I'm sure there were many more scattered around the ground.

It was becoming evident to me that there was something more than football linking these people. Perhaps this communal feeling was almost a celebration of their shared hardship. If you are being honest, the vast majority of Celtic supporters are Catholics or people who come from a Catholic background.

These are the descendants of Irish immigrants who had come to Scotland, a country where they were not particularly made to feel welcome.

It is almost an ethnic minority thing; it was 'us' against 'them' and if they could feel safe and wanted by gathering to follow a football team, was it any surprise that people got excited supporting Celtic Football Club?

The Stein era and the achievement of winning nine Scottish league championships in a row turned the football club into an institution; it also heaped enormous pressure on Celtic players who were to follow. We will always be measured against those successes.

But interestingly, I experienced the same bond of togetherness when Bernadette and I went to Lourdes two months after our wedding. The Celtic Supporters Association paid for the trip after hearing Father O'Keeffe say that we planned to make the pilgrimage to the place of miracles.

Here were all these people with such enduring faith coming to this place in France, walking through caves and touching waters in the hope that something remarkable might happen.

It's often said of Lourdes that people don't necessarily come back cured; but they tend to be much more spiritually at ease with themselves. I will cherish the memories of the two of us, just walking hand-in-hand through all the people filled with hope.

There are some terribly ill souls there – folk getting pushed along in mobile beds and wheelchairs. It is very humbling to go to a place like that.

We didn't take part in the processions. We would go to the Grotto every night and I would push a little prayer of my own into the crack on the wall. We liked to sit on a wall and watch it all go by, listening to people singing 'Ave Maria'. Time just seemed to stand still.

We bought ourselves a map to find out where the baths were with the healing waters. Bernadette had been on her chemotherapy so her energy levels were really quite good.

We found 'Baths' marked on the map and began to walk. It must have been two miles to these baths, right through the shrine and up the high street, full of shops selling all the statues of Our Lady.

When we got there, we discovered we had walked to the

public swimming baths, complete with diving board and lifeguard. We sat down and laughed our heads off. And walked the two miles back again.

Much later, after her health had deteriorated, we even consulted a faith healer, a chap in Dublin called Cyril Childs. Bernadette's dad, who is Irish, knew of someone who had achieved success by going to see this man, so we thought it was worth a try.

We flew to Dublin and checked into a hotel near the rugby ground in Lansdowne Road for the four days we would be there. By this time, Bernie couldn't really walk, so we stayed in the hotel for most of the time and we'd take a taxi for the six sessions with Mr Childs.

I am a real fan of Dublin. I've been there loads of times and I love walking around the shops and sampling the atmosphere south of the river in Grafton Street.

But Bernie just wasn't up to it, so rather than even facing a walk downstairs to the restaurant, we would stay in our room and order room service.

Mr Childs is a farmer who apparently discovered his powers late in life; a very down-to-earth sort of bloke who very quickly put us at our ease. It was not a case of Mr Childs laying his hands on Bernadette; he would place his big shovel hands over her body. There was some form of magnetism coming out of those hands because you could see the hairs on the body rising as he placed them over her.

He would only have to lay his hand on your forehead and you would feel yourself tipping backwards.

But I don't know if we got anything out of it. What I do know is that it was one further avenue of hope that we could not afford to ignore.

I had never been at all religious; prior to coming to Scotland, my church appearances were limited to things like christenings, when you would have no more than 10 people in the place.

All of a sudden, you are in a country where hundreds of thousands of people are attending mass, all together, singing the same songs and knowing every response to the priest's words.

At St John's in Barrhead and St Charles's in Paisley, you struggle to get a seat at Sunday Mass. The unity of the people, from all walks of life, was awe-inspiring.

I sit sometimes, and wonder whether I should now turn to Catholicism. Not simply for the religious aspect, but also for the comfort of immersing myself in people who genuinely seem to care about you. It's just a closer-knit religion than anything I had known before.

Footballers are not exactly steeped in the tradition of going to church, I know. I can think of a few blokes I have known in my career who could not think of a more tiresome chore.But having been introduced to it by Bernadette and her family, I find the occasion serene and comforting.

I don't know how big a ceremony it is to become a Catholic but I just think it would be nice to line up with the other people and take the bread and wine of Holy Communion.

Religion must be right. If there is not a God in heaven – and this isn't just a Catholic belief – then what are we all here for? What is our purpose in life? Are we just to live on the earth for 70 years and die?

What is the point in striving to lead a good life if you are not trying to win a place in heaven with the Lord?

The tragic loss in March of this year of former Ranger Davie Cooper just goes to show how everyone must be ready for death, every day of their life. You have to live each day of your life as if it was your last and to live it in the fashion that you would want to be remembered.

Even in his final days, Davie Cooper was a player feared by Celtic's fans and players alike. That's why the supporters singled him out for special treatment whenever he was playing.

I can think of no greater compliment to a player of 39 years than that, had we faced Clydebank instead of Airdrie in the final of the 1995 Scottish Cup, I am sure Coop would have been singled out by our gaffer as the side's real danger man.

Unfortunately, I didn't see him at his peak with Rangers. I played against him a couple of times when he played for Motherwell. He was by then 36 years old but you could still see he had great feet.

You never knew if he was coming inside you or outside, such was his ability to deceive. If that was what he was like in the winter of his career, I shudder to think what heights he hit in the spring and summer.

From what people tell me and the tapes I've seen of him in action, I'm sure that, had he left Scotland, he would have achieved a reputation comparable to Kenny Dalglish. He was something special.

I am sufficiently convinced of the hereafter that I will live the rest of my life in the manner I have lived it up to now: to try to be a good person to ensure that one day, I am back in soul with Bernadette. Because I know for a fact she is there, and there's nothing I'll do in my life to jeopardise that meeting.

Even in the last few weeks, I've felt her presence in my loneliness and despair.

I'll come home from training and there's just the dog here. Then I look at my pictures, I've got them in almost every room in the house, and they give me an inner strength.

I feel like breaking down to cry sometimes. What am I going to do with my life? I've, perhaps, got 50 years left in me. How am I going to get through it? But then I find there is something within me, urging me to be strong, not to cry, telling me to get on with my life, it's O.K.

And if that's not Bernadette, I don't know what it is.

Her presence is with me all the time. I talk to her when I'm alone in the car. When it came to debating over a new contract with Celtic, I would ask Bernie what she thought.

I have decided that for the next year, at least, I would like to be around Glasgow. I visit her grave every day and maintain a strong and loving relationship with her family.

She's even physically close to me now, since I have had her wedding ring and engagement ring forged into one. And I'll wear it always on my right hand, even during games.

Men of the cloth have been a great comfort to me, both before and after Bernadette's death. We forged a special relationship with Father O'Keeffe. When I think of the way he comforted Bernie when she broke down in his little office, it was almost the way a grandfather would.

And Father Dominic Towey, from St John Ogilvie Parish in Blantyre, could also soothe and relax us with his words. We'd sit there, among the burning candles and he'd touch Bernadette with the oils and pray for the miracle to happen. And always, that deep, soothing voice trying to wash our heartache away.

On the day Bernie passed away, my father-in-law Jimmy Doyle came up to the bedroom. He said to me: 'The Cardinal is downstairs. He would like to see you.'

Cardinal Thomas Winning had only been elevated by the Pope a month before. Yet he could find time to speak to us in our hour of need.

Again, his words almost made things seem right. We all went upstairs and Cardinal Winning said a little Mass. Your wife had only passed away about two hours ago . . . she was laid there right in front of you. Yet you were being swept along into a feeling of relaxation by a man's words.

Yes, it was true that she was now out of pain and there was something to be taken from that.

The only time I could not agree with Cardinal Winning was when he said Bernadette was now in a better place, in Paradise. He said we should be pleased for her because she was looking down on us from the place she'd rather be.

I may be no cardinal but I know Bernadette would never want

164

to be with anyone rather than me. Even with God. I know He could do no more for her or make my Bernadette any happier than I could.

You see, I knew what we had together.

*If you would like to make a donation to the
Beatson Oncology Centre Fund,
the cancer charity supported by Tony Mowbray,
please send what you can to:
Dr. A.G. Robertson, Treasurer, The Beatson
Oncology Centre Fund, The Beatson Oncology
centre, Western Infirmary, Glasgow G11 6NT*